"The ecclesiology of William Perkins is a neglected field of study in historical theology. With careful analysis of Perkins's works—including from his sermons, expositions, and theological treatises—Justin Miller helps fill that gap and lays a foundation for further discussion by investigating Perkins's understanding of worship, the local church, the sacraments, hermeneutics, preaching, and poimenics."

–Joel R. Beeke, chancellor, Puritan Reformed Theological Seminary

"Justin Miller calls Christians, and pastors especially, to hold true to the priorities of biblical Reformed Christianity in the local church, as modelled in the thought of William Perkins and the Reformed tradition through the centuries. What shines forth is Perkins's love for the triune God and his people, and how that love came to expression in pastoral doctrines which are equally relevant today as they were in Perkins's time."

–Matthew Payne, director, Stretch

"William Perkins is an ideal guide on the topics of church and pastoral ministry for a variety of reasons. His convictions were biblically fixed, yet warmly expressed. His position promoted unity, and in this stance he was unshakeable. His exhortations were simple, yet gloriously Christ-centered. This work will be of value to any who seek to deepen their roots in these matters."

–J. D. Edwards, preaching pastor, Reformed Heritage Church

"William Perkins is considered by many to be the 'father of the Puritans.' Justin Miller has mined the treasure trove of Perkins's pastoral theology and returned with much spiritual gold, which he now shares with you all. Written in a lively and accessible style, and eminently practical, it is my prayer that ministers will learn from this 'Giant of Cambridge' how to be more useful in the Lord's vineyard."

–Todd Ruddell, pastor, Christ Covenant Reformed Presbyterian Church

William Perkins on Pastoral Theology

WILLIAM PERKINS ON PASTORAL THEOLOGY

—— Justin Miller ——

RESOURCE *Publications* • Eugene, Oregon

WILLIAM PERKINS ON PASTORAL THEOLOGY

Copyright © 2023 Justin Miller. All rights reserved. Except for brief quotations in critical publications or reviews, no part of this book may be reproduced in any manner without prior written permission from the publisher. Write: Permissions, Wipf and Stock Publishers, 199 W. 8th Ave., Suite 3, Eugene, OR 97401.

Resource Publications
An Imprint of Wipf and Stock Publishers
199 W. 8th Ave., Suite 3
Eugene, OR 97401

www.wipfandstock.com

PAPERBACK ISBN: 979-8-3852-0008-5
HARDCOVER ISBN: 979-8-3852-0619-3
EBOOK ISBN: 979-8-3852-0620-9

VERSION NUMBER 11/28/23

CONTENTS

Acknowledgments | vii

CHAPTER 1: PERKINS' LIFE AND THOUGHT | 1
    A brief biographical survey of the life of William Perkins 2
    A consideration of Church Fathers and Perkins 6
    Some thoughts on the Fathers for today's pastors 10

CHAPTER 2: PERKINS' VIEW OF THE LOCAL CHURCH | 12
    The Church from Perkins' perspective 14
    The local church 17
    The imperative of the worship of God in the local church 23
    What about the Lord's Day as the Christian Sabbath? 24
    What was required of professors to be part of the local church? 27
    Conclusion 30

CHAPTER 3: INTRODUCTION TO PERKINS' VIEW OF THE SACRAMENTS | 33
    Proper use of sacraments 37

CONTENTS

CHAPTER 4: PERKINS' VIEW OF BAPTISM | 40
    Mode of baptism   44
    Conclusion of Perkins' thought on baptism   47

**CHAPTER 5: PERKINS' VIEW OF
THE LORD'S SUPPER | 49**
    Roman Catholic and Protestant views of
    the Lord's Supper   50
    Conclusion of Perkins' thought on the Lord's Supper   55

**CHAPTER 6: PERKINS' VIEW OF
PASTORAL MINISTRY | 59**
    An educated clergy   63
    Pastors must know the flock they are charged
    to care for   65
    Pastors protect the flock   69
    Conclusion of Perkins' thought on pastoral ministry   71

**CHAPTER 7: PERKINS' VIEW OF
PASTORAL PREACHING | 74**
    Perkins' understanding of the imperative of preaching   77
    What exactly is preaching?   79
    Interpretation of Scripture   83
    Prayer and proclamation   84
    The responsibility of a pastor to study   86
    The responsibility of the people to listen   89
    Conclusion   93

CHAPTER 8: CONCLUSION | 95

Bibliography | 101

ACKNOWLEDGMENTS

To Christ my King. All fades in comparison to Your majestic glory. You are worth living for and dying for.

To my wife JoDawn, you are a great gift from God to an unworthy man.

To my kids, I pray that you savor Christ Jesus all your days.

To Dr. Todd Ruddell, thank you for your wisdom, encouragement, and exhortation in this and all things pastoral theology.

To Pastor Buddy Clinton, thank you for your encouragement to finish the doctoral degree and your friendship in life and ministry.

To my church family, God has graciously allowed me to serve you these years for Christ Jesus' glory.

Chapter One

PERKINS' LIFE AND THOUGHT

I HAVE HEARD IT often stated, "Those who do not learn from history are doomed to repeat it." [1] The idea is that history grants perspective for the present time in such a way that it can prevent mistakes from being repeated. The study of history can be a great tool God uses to shape men for more faithful ministry that will withstand the cultural fads and trends of their time. Charles Bridges, in his book *The Christian Ministry*, writes:

> "The Great Head of the Church had ordained three grand repositories of his truth. In the Scriptures he has preserved it by his Providence against all hostile attacks. In the hearts of Christians he has maintained it by the Almighty energy of his Spirit—even under every outward token of general apostacy. And in the Christian Ministry he has deposited 'the treasure in earthen vessels' for the edification and enriching of the Church in successive ages." [2]

Bridges conveys three repositories and identifies the Christian ministry as one of those, seeing the ministry as a gift of God to

---

1. This quotation is often attributed to writer and philosopher George Santayana.
2. Bridges, Charles. *The Christian Ministry*. The Banner of Truth Trust. Carlisle, Pennsylvania. 1967, 2.

the Church for her flourishing and well-being. If what Bridges said is correct, then it is imperative for the Gospel Ministry to learn from history so as not to repeat mistakes, yet also to strive in good conscience to repeat biblical faithfulness in the examples we read. Remember the old adage, "You can see further down the way when you stand on someone's shoulders." With this in view, we are going to examine one of the first Puritans and his view of pastoral ministry to glean from his insights on how to carry on this great calling and perform this office to the glory of God. We want to stand on his shoulders to see more clearly and perhaps further on the topics of pastoral ministry, the local church, the sacraments, and preaching. The Christian minister is presented as a gift from God in Ephesians 4:7-15 for gathering the elect of God, their maturation toward holiness, for their growth in service of others, and for the edification of the body of believers. The pastor exists to teach the people of God to put off the old man and put on the new man (Ephesians 4:20-24). Therefore, this great gift of Christ should be explored for the good of the churches of our time. What better source to go to for this study than one whom some would label "the father of the Puritans," namely, William Perkins.

A brief biographical survey of the life of William Perkins

William Perkins was born in Marston Jabbet, Warwickshire, in 1558, and he died in 1602 in his early 40s.[3] He had a reputation for drunkenness and wild living in his earlier years. According to J.I. Packer, he studied at Christ's College Cambridge with Laurence Chaderton as his tutor. He was converted, and a passion for theology replaced his previous interests in astrological studies and loose living. In 1584 he graduated with his MA and soon after became

---

3. The information in this section is available via public domain. See the following works: Beeke, Joel R. and Greg Salazar, eds. *William Perkins: Architect of Puritanism*. Grand Rapids, Michigan. Reformation Heritage Books. 2019. Packer, J.I. *Puritan Portraits*. Christian Focus. Fearn, Ross-shire. United Kingdom. 2012, 129.

a fellow at Cambridge and a lecturer at Great St. Andrews, which according to Packer, was a poor and needy parish. Perkins, though a lecturer, carried with him a pastoral heart toward the needs of those to whom he ministered. A taste of Perkins' pastoral heart can be seen by sampling titles of many of his writings. He outlined how man was to speak in *Direction for Government of Tongue*, the danger of witchcraft in *Damned Art of Witchcraft*, everyday living in *Treatise on How to Live Well in All Estates*, how one ought to prosecute his occupation in *Treatise on Vocation*, the family in *Right Manner of Erecting and Ordering a Family*, and even addressed prognostication in *Resolution to Countrymen on Prognostication*. His writing and sermons included much practicality.

In his position at Cambridge, Perkins influenced Puritans such as William Ames, John Robinson, Thomas Goodwin, Paul Baynes, Samuel Ward, Phineas Fletcher, Thomas Draxe, Richard Sibbes, Thomas Hooker, John Cotton, and Thomas Shepard. He influenced far more people with his writings, such as *The Golden Chain* and *Art of Prophesying*. Packer writes:

> "The name of William Perkins is hardly known today outside a small circle of professional historians and theologians. It may therefore come as a surprise to learn that during the half-century from 1585 to 1635, Perkins was far and away the best-known and best-selling English writer of Christian books for ordinary people. More than that, he was the best-known English international theologian, being classed with Calvin and Beza as third in what someone called 'the trinity of orthodox.' But so indeed he was. It is a fact that almost ninety editions of works by him were published in translation in the Netherlands, fifty plus in both Switzerland and Germany, and smaller printings in half a dozen other languages." [4]

Much of modern scholarship agrees with Packer's summary of Perkins' influence. Muller points out the influence that Perkins had. He writes in *Christ and Decree*:

---

4. Packer, J.I. *Puritan Portraits*. Christian Focus. Fearn, Ross-shire. United Kingdom. 2012, 129.

> "William Perkins (1558-1602) was perhaps the most eminent English Reformed theologian of the late sixteenth century, everywhere recognized, along with Peter Martyr Vermigli, Theodore Beza, Lambert Daneau, and William Ames, as a major exponent of Reformed theology. Heinrich Heppe viewed Perkins as a 'father of pietism' and characterized that most casual of Perkins' treatises, A Golden Chain, as a study of the ground of piety and of holy living." [5]

According to Muller, in his book Grace and Freedom:

> "Perkins has been variously identified in scholarship as a distinctly English churchman and prominent apologist of the Church of England, a 'father of Puritanism,' or, alternatively, of Pietism, an exponent of early Reformed orthodoxy, a supralapsarian Calvinist, and one among several ancestors of the anti-Arminian line of English theology in the early modern era." [6]

Muller cites various sources to confirm his thesis on Perkins' influence. Perkins was a towering figure in his time, yet the study of his works, in comparison to work done on other Puritans, has not been reviewed at length in our day.

Perkins' thought heavily revolved around doctrines such as predestination, justification, sanctification, the proper understanding of the attributes of God, and the sinful state of man. This was, of course, a Reformed emphasis. According to Dewey Wallace, Reformed preachers emphasized proper doctrine and practice. He writes, "Distinct within the Reformed teaching about grace and predestination, and related to predestination as its end, was an emphasis upon sanctification by the regenerating force of the Holy Spirit."[7] Wallace points out the emphasis unique

---

5. Muller, Richard A. *Christ and Decree: Christology and Predestination from Calvin to Perkins*. Grand Rapids, Michigan: Baker Academic. 2008, 131.

6. Muller, Richard A. *Grace and Freedom. William Perkins and the Early Modern Reformed Understanding of Divine Grace and Free Will*. Oxford, England. Oxford University Press. 2020, 9.

7. Wallace, Jr., Dewey D. *Puritans and Predestination: Grace in English Protestant Theology*, 1525-1695 (Eugene, Ore.: Wipf & Stock Publishers, 1982), 7.

to Reformed scholarship, which drove Perkins' thought not only on theology proper but also on ecclesiology, which shaped and informed his view of pastoral ministry. We read this also in the writings of men like Calvin, who vigorously put forth the reality of the Gospel conveyed and preached as the means God uses to grant and strengthen faith. Calvin writes:

> "That since there remains nothing for men, as to themselves, but to perish, being smitten by the just judgment of God, they are to be justified freely through his mercy; for Christ comes to the aid of this misery, and communicates himself to believers, so that they find in him alone all those things in which they are wanting. There is perhaps, no passage (speaking of Romans 3:24) in the whole of Scripture which illustrates in a more striking manner the efficacy of his righteousness; for it shows that God's mercy is the efficient cause, that Christ with his blood is the meritorious cause, that the formal or instrumental cause is faith in the word, and that, moreover, the final cause is the glory of the divine justice and goodness."[8]

Calvin understood rightly that works could not bring one to God, nor could law-keeping or ceremonial acts. No pope, cardinal, bishop, or council could grant salvation; only God, through His Gospel, embraced by faith. This truth was carried forward after Calvin by men such as Perkins. Remember, as mentioned above, the influence of Perkins and how he built on the teaching of Luther, Calvin, and Beza. Perkins, in his time, began to displace Calvin, Beza, and Bullinger at the end of the sixteenth century as the most-read reformed theologian. [9]

According to Ian Breward, William Perkins was the first English theological writer to gain an audience spread over many

---

8. Calvin, John. *Romans. Calvin's Commentaries.* Translated from the original Latin by the Reverend William Pringle. Grand Rapids, Michigan. 1981. Volume XIX., 141.

9. See Ballitch, Andrew. The reference is: Ballitch, Andrew S. *Not to Behold Faith, But the Object of Faith: The Effect of William Perkins's Doctrine of the Atonement on his Preaching of Assurance.* Themelios, Volume 40. Issue 3.

countries outside the magisterial Reformers.[10] Now, while Perkins' theology was developing beyond Calvin, it was, like the Genevan Master, heavily influenced by the best of Patristic teaching, as I hope briefly now to demonstrate.

A consideration of the Church Fathers and Perkins

Now while I do not intend to exhaust this topic, as it would be a dissertation of its own *and a worthy one*, a sample of citations by Perkins from his writings gives ample evidence of the great influence the Fathers had on his thought and ministry. In Perkins' work entitled *A Discourse on Conscience*, Perkins references Tertullian's work on the Christian conscience in the faith *Apol. cap.9.Lib.de Pudicitia*:

> "Indeed, Tertullian says plainly that Christians in his days abstained from eating of blood, and he persuades men to continue in so doing because he is of opinion that this very law of the apostles must last to the end of the world." [11]

Perkins, in this same work, goes on immediately to reference Origen in the work *Contra Cels.lib.8*: "Origen says that this law was very necessary in his days," as well as Augustine's work when he writes, "Augustine says that it is a good thing to abstain from things offered to idols, though it is in necessity." [12] These citations make it clear that Perkins had great familiarity with these fathers

10. See Breward, Ian. *The Significance of William Perkins*. JRH 4. 1996.113-116. That was referenced in the following article: Ballitch, Andrew S. *Not to Behold Faith, But the Object of Faith: The Effect of William Perkins's Doctrine of the Atonement on his Preaching of Assurance.* Themelios, Volume 40. Issue 3.

11. See Perkins, William. *Discourse on Conscience*. Vol. 8 of *The Works of William Perkins*. Edited by J. Stephen Yuille. General Editors Joel R. Beeke and Derek W.H. Thomas. Grand Rapids, Michigan. Reformation Heritage Books. 2019, 29.

12. See Origen and Augustine in: Perkins, William. *Discourse on Conscience*. Vol. 8 of *The Works of William Perkins*. Edited by J. Stephen Yuille. General Editors Joel R. Beeke and Derek W.H. Thomas. Grand Rapids, Michigan. Reformation Heritage Books. 2019, 29.

and their writings. Later he will quote Irenaeus in his epistle to Victor, which he read in Eusebius. He writes:

> *"Irenaeus, in his epistle to Victor, cited by Eusebius, says, 'Some have thought that they must fast one day, some two days, some more, some forty hours day and night, which diversity of fasting commends the unity of faith.'"* [13]

He goes on to reference Eusebius and summarizes him when he states, "And Eusebius records that Montanus, the heretic, was the first that prescribed solemn and set laws of fasting."[14] Here we have both a direct quotation by Perkins and a summation of Eusebius' teachings.

A few other examples will help to solidify our point. In his work, *The Third Book of the Cases of Conscience,* he refers both to Chrysostom and Ambrose. He writes: "And, therefore, to them who shall condemn fit and convenient recreation (as some of the ancient fathers have done, by name Chrysostom and Ambrose), it may be said, 'Be not too righteousness, be not too wise.'" [15] In his *Second Book on Cases of Conscience,* he writes, referencing Cyril, Chrysostom, and Augustine:

> *"Third, Christ and His apostles kept the first day of the week as the Sabbath. For Christ rose again the first day of the week, and appeared to His disciples and eight days after, He appeared again to Thomas, which was the next first day of the week. And this has been the opinion of sundry and ancient divines. Cyril (Cyril.1.11. in Joh.c.58),*

---

13. See Perkins, William. *Discourse on Conscience. Vol. 8 of The Works of William Perkins.* Edited by J. Stephen Yuille. General Editors Joel R. Beeke and Derek W.H. Thomas. Grand Rapids, Michigan. Reformation Heritage Books. 2019, 33.

14. See Perkins, William. *Discourse on Conscience. Vol. 8 of The Works of William Perkins.* Edited by J. Stephen Yuille. General Editors Joel R. Beeke and Derek W.H. Thomas. Grand Rapids, Michigan. Reformation Heritage Books. 2019, 33-34.

15. See Perkins, William. *Three Books on Cases of Conscience. Vol. 8 of The Works of William Perkins.* Edited by J. Stephen Yuille. General Editors Joel R. Beeke and Derek W.H. Thomas. Grand Rapids, Michigan. Reformation Heritage Books. 2019, 416.

upon John, says that this eighth day was without doubt the Lord's day, and so ought to be kept because it is likely Christ Himself kept it holy. And the same is affirmed and taught by Augustine (Ad Casulanum. Epist. 86. ad Januarium. Epist. 119. c. 13) and Chrysostom (Serm.5 de resurrect)."[16]

He later states, "Therefore, it was prescribed to be kept the eighth day. Thus, the ancient fathers, by name Cyprian and Augustine, have reasoned and taught."[17] Notice that he is appealing to the fathers to prove his position on the Sabbath as well as the Christian conscience. He was formulating his theology not apart from the Fathers but in his reading of them in light of the Holy Scripture. He was standing on their shoulders to see what they saw and perhaps to understand more clearly than they did. You can find in his discourse on the conscience references to Theodoret and Aquinas as well as further references to Augustine and Chrysostom, among others.[18]

In his work, *The Protasis*, Perkins references Basil, Hilary, Ambrose, and Jerome. He calls them the "learned fathers." He writes:

> "In the first sense alone faith justifies and saves, and nothing else within us. To this do the learned fathers agree. Basil (Hom.de humil. Fide sola in Christum se justifcari) says, 'This perfect rejoicing in God, when a man is not puffed up for his own justice, but acknowledges that he wants justice, and that he is justified by faith alone in Christ.' Hilary: 'That is remitted of Christ by faith, which

---

16. See Perkins, William. *Three Books on Cases of Conscience.* Vol. 8 of *The Works of William Perkins.* Edited by J. Stephen Yuille. General Editors Joel R. Beeke and Derek W.H. Thomas. Grand Rapids, Michigan. Reformation Heritage Books. 2019, 348.

17. See Perkins, William. *Three Books on Cases of Conscience.* Vol. 8 of *The Works of William Perkins.* Edited by J. Stephen Yuille. General Editors Joel R. Beeke and Derek W.H. Thomas. Grand Rapids, Michigan. Reformation Heritage Books. 2019, 348.

18. See Perkins, William. *Discourse on Conscience.* Vol. 8 of *The Works of William Perkins.* Edited by J. Stephen Yuille. General Editors Joel R. Beeke and Derek W.H. Thomas. Grand Rapids, Michigan. Reformation Heritage Books. 2019, 69, 75.

> *the law could not loosen, for faith alone justifies.' Ambrose (in cap 3. Ad. Rom. Nihil operates): 'They are justified freely which do nothing, nor repay like for like, are justified by faith alone, through the gift of God.' Again, in his commentary upon the epistle to the Corinthians: 'This is appointed of God, that he who believes in Christ should be saved without works, by faith alone receiving remission of sins.' Jerome: 'God justifieth by faith alone.'"* [19]

In that same section, he continues his citations, quoting Bernard, Lactantius, and Chrysostom as well as referencing "hundreds places of fathers":

> "Bernard (Libro de gratia & lib. Arbitrio. Via regni non causa regnandi) well said that works are 'the way to the kingdom of heaven and not the causes of reigning.' Lactantius (Epit.divin.institute.c.9.) says, 'Great is the help of repentance, which, whosoever takes away, cuts off to himself the way of life.' Chrysostom (Homil. 38 in John): 'Some by watching, by sleeping on the bare ground, by toiling their bodies with daily labor do blot out their sins: but you may obtain the same by a more easy way, that is by forgiving.' Thus many hundreds places of fathers are to be understood, when they ascribe remission of sins to martyrdom, fasting, prayer, works of mercy, and such like."[20]

What is clear in all these citations and references is Perkins' theology of justification by grace alone through faith alone in Christ alone, as well as his view of Christian liberty and life was developed not apart from the fathers but in reference and study of the fathers in light of Holy Scripture. Think of all the references briefly mentioned thus far. We have quotations or summations of Ambrose, Augustine, Aquinas, Basil, Bernard, Chrysostom, Hilary, Eusebius, Jerome, and Tertullian, to name some of his sources. He calls them the "learned fathers," those who knew the doctrines of the faith and were entrusted to preach them to the Church. He

---

19. Perkins, William. *The Protasis*. Vol. 9 of *The Works of William Perkins*. Edited by J. Stephen Yuille. General Editors Joel R. Beeke and Derek W.H. Thomas. Grand Rapids, Michigan. Reformation Heritage Books. 2020, 37.

20. Ibid., 37-38.

looked to them and argued from their teachings for them to inform his own understanding of the Word and ways of God. His view of justification and the Sabbath was codified in conjunction with the Patristic teaching from Scripture. Perkins was, in many ways, a bridge from the Fathers to the times of the English Puritan movement. He put forth clearly, and precisely those truths defended and died for in previous generations. One such set of teachings he was diligent to convey was his understanding of pastoral ministry and its wide influence on the life of a local church.

Some thoughts on the Fathers for today's pastors

One of the greatest tragedies in the modern church has been the negligence of the study of the early Church fathers. At this point, it is important to note that the Patristic Fathers and their study was clearly an endeavor Perkins undertook, and it shaped his theological conclusions in a great way. Would it not be a worthwhile endeavor for us today in our modern church context? Surely it would. Studying the Patristic Fathers would help us to see the difference between the apostolic-inspired Scriptures and the Fathers who followed them. It would give us a greater appreciation of what the apostles put forth, inspired by God. In addition, it would help us immensely in our time of shallow doctrine to read their writing on Christology, the sacraments, and the Church. We have much to learn from them.

Much of the study of Scripture in the denomination I was a part of was done without consideration of the Church Fathers and their works. I was unaware and untrained in much of what they argued for and stood for. The discovery process for certain doctrines and practices would have been greatly helped if I had been exposed to such writings earlier. There is a rich heritage of teaching and literature we have as Christians that in our modern time goes untouched, to our own weakening, as people who profess to hold to the once and for all delivered apostolic deposit (Jude 3). These men were gifts to the Church (Ephesians 4:11-14), and we are to stand on their shoulders, thereby seeing farther than what they did. This is one of the great privileges we have with regard to the studying of Scripture. We can read Augustine and Chrysostom and others to glean their insights from Scripture. It is our heritage in Christ. How much more strength, theologically speaking, would I have had as a pastor caring for a flock of Christ, if I had been given access to the Patristic Fathers at the beginning of my ministry? Reading them critically, yes, but learning from them and their love of the Thrice Holy God from the Scripture. May God grant that the church visible, which today is filled with so much pragmatism, would instead be filled with more historical theology for God's glory and the church's good.

— Chapter Two —

PERKINS' VIEW OF THE LOCAL CHURCH

PAUL, IN HIS PRAYER in Ephesians 3:20-21 states, "Now to him who is able to do far more abundantly than all that we ask or think, according to the power at work within us, to him *be glory in the church and in Christ Jesus* throughout all generations, forever and ever. Amen." (emphasis added) Paul, in his prayer, acknowledges that God is glorified in the church and in Christ Jesus. The church is where God is glorified the greatest on earth. It is the primary place we see God's manifold wisdom on display. It is the apple of His eye in Christ Jesus our Lord. The universal Church, which is manifested locally, is the very institution that the Lord Jesus Christ Himself promised to build against which the gates of Hades would never prevail. Our Lord Jesus stated, "And I tell you, you are Peter, and on this rock I will build my church, and the gates of hell shall not prevail against it" (Matthew 16:18). Christ Jesus builds His Church. The Church here is the final gathering of His redeemed from every tribe, tongue, and nation. Christ is the head of the Church. Colossians 1:18: "And he is the head of the body, the church. He is the beginning, the firstborn from the dead, that in everything he might be preeminent." The Church is Christ's body on earth.

PERKINS' VIEW OF THE LOCAL CHURCH

The Greek word *ekklēsia* is the common word used in the New Testament to describe the church. It is used 114 times in the New Testament, with a broad range of meanings. In some contexts, it indicates all God's people redeemed from all time (invisible Church), as well as all God's professing people in the world or God's professing people in a region, and in many contexts, the local gathering of God's professing people in a place, or under one government, as the "church" in Jerusalem, Antioch, etc. For example, Ephesians 5:23, 25 and Hebrews 12:23 refer to the invisible Church, which is the elect of God from all time. In Romans 16:5, as well as Colossians 4:15, the word is used of the professing visible church in a location that meets together as a covenanted community of professors. As an institution created by God and maintained to the end of the age, it is no wonder that this church is the centerpiece of God's work in the world. It is also no wonder that it was the focal point of Puritan life and thought. Puritans deeply concerned about the true and pure worship of God were naturally concerned about the local church and desired to regulate her functions according to Holy Scripture. John Owen, a Puritan who would follow after Perkins and stand on his shoulders, writes this:

> *"Holiness becometh the house of the Lord for ever; without it none shall see God. Christ died to wash his church, to present it before his Father without spot or blemish; to purchase unto himself a peculiar people, zealous for good works. It is the kingdom of God within us, and by which it appeared unto all that we are children of the kingdom. Let this, then, be the great discriminating character of the church from the world, that they are holy, humbled, self-denying people. Our Master is holy; his doctrine and worship are holy; Let us strive that our hearts may also be holy."* [1]

Owen, like all the Puritans, was a churchman and saw the visible church as the place where God's glory was on display in

---

1. Owen, John. *Eschol, A Cluster of the Fruit of Canaan: Mutual Duties of a Church Fellowship.* Vol. 13. of *The Works of John Owen.* (ed. William H. Goold. London: The Banner of Truth Trust. 1983), 64.

the greatest way in this world, for she is, as Owen said, whom "Christ died to wash" to present before the Father "without spot or blemish." Owen made it clear that the church should be clearly distinct from the world in which she lived. A distinct people. A separate people. Perkins, before Owen, had similar things to say about the church visible and church local. He was concerned with the worship of the visible local church and who its members were to be. As a lecturer at St. Andrews, he saw many who had no fruit of conversion and no true claim to the church yet were treated as though they were indeed Christian simply because of being a citizen of England in a parish system.

The Church from Perkins' perspective

Perkins' exposition of the visible church (universal, regional, and local) was not as polished as someone like Owen, who addresses the issue of particularly the local church at a time that these doctrines were being clarified. However, Perkins does deal with the visible universal Church and the visible local church at various points in his writings. Perkins, in his work on the Lord's Prayer, describes the kingdom of God, as he calls it, as follows:

> *"In a kingdom, there are four things to be noted: (1) there must be a king; (2) there must be subjects; (3) there are laws; (4) authority. In this kingdom, Christ is the King. It is He to whom the Father has given all authority in heaven and earth. In this kingdom, all are not subjects but such as are willing to give free and frank obedience to God's Word or, at the least, though their hearts be not so sound, make an outward profession of it. The laws of this kingdom are the Word of God in the books of the Old and New Testaments . . . The power and authority is that whereby Christ converts effectually those which are to be converted by the inward operation of His Spirit and glorifies Himself in the confusion of the rest."* [2]

---

2. Perkins, William. *An Exposition of the Lord's Prayer*. Vol. 5 of *The Works of William Perkins*. Edited by Ryan Hurd. General Editors Joel R. Beeke and Derek W.H. Thomas. Grand Rapids, Michigan. Reformation Heritage Books.

PERKINS' VIEW OF THE LOCAL CHURCH

Perkins outlined the universal visible church with the biblical imagery of a kingdom with a king, laws, and citizens. According to Perkins, the kingdom of God has Christ as King, God's Word as the laws of the people, and its citizens are those who profess the truth deposited by the apostles. Perkins believed the universal visible Church to be those who, unlike Rome as of 1563 with Trent, confessed the true apostolic doctrine of the Gospel.

Perkins viewed the local church as where both the elect were drawn and the reprobate hardened at the authentic preaching of the Gospel, when he wrote, "Whereby Christ converts effectually those which are converted by the inward operation of His Spirit and glorifies Himself in the confusion of the rest."[3] This view of Perkins is in direct contrast, to some degree, to the idea that the church on earth was an institution that granted salvation. This is an important distinction, for Rome had departed from the faith in the Council of Trent, thereby leaving the true visible Church of God on earth. Perkins rejected Rome's view of the church, with the papacy being the uniting factor of all congregations and groups. Perkins writes in *The Epistle Dedicatory*:

> *"Among the many reasons which have persuaded me that popery cannot be the true religion, this is not the least: the insufficiency of their doctrine of faith and repentance. These two things, though they are the chief and principal points in religion, and so necessary that he who does not but know and practice them aright can never be saved, yet I dare avouch that the faith and repentance of the Romish church, as they are taught by many of the best approved papists, are no better than such a faith and such a repentance as a hypocrite and a very reprobate may attain unto."* [4]

Perkins viewed the popery of the Romish church as outside the faith once and for all delivered. Perkins saw the Roman

---

2017, 443.

3. Ibid., 443.

4. Perkins, William. *The Epistle Dedicatory*. Edited by J. Stephen Yuille. General Editors Joel R. Beeke and Derek W.H. Thomas. Grand Rapids, Michigan. Reformation Heritage Books. 2020, 81.

church as having the Pope as its head, thereby denying the Kingship/Headship of the Lord Jesus. He saw the Roman church's citizenry as being those who united under a false head instead of those who made a valid profession of faith in the biblical Gospel under Christ's rule administered through His established leadership. The majority of those in Rome, according to Perkins, were not and are not part of the redeemed of God. They were part of a false church that had broken off, in the Catholic Reformation of Trent, from the true catholic (universal) visible Church. He would have abhorred much of the "Catholics-and-Protestants-together" language, so prevalent in our modern era.

Perkins saw the Church and its proper doctrine as crucial to the health generationally of the visible church both particularly and throughout the world (universal). Perkins made it clear that the apostolic deposit given from Jesus must be passed down rightly. He writes:

> "Christ taught that which He heard of the Father; the apostles, that which they heard of Christ: ordinary ministers, that which they learned of the apostles. This is the right tradition. And it be observed without addition or detraction, the gospel shall remain in its integrity. Here our ancestors are greatly to be blamed, who have not contented themselves with that which they have learned of the apostles, but have delivered things of their own which they were never taught. Hence sprang unwritten traditions, and the corruption of religion." [5]

When the truths of Scripture and doctrines of the apostles were not taught rightly and distortions to the Gospel were made by Rome, Perkins conveyed that corruption and spiritual death was the default position of the members of such an institution labeled "church."

---

5. Perkins, William. *Commentary on Galatians. Vol. 2 of The Works of William Perkins.* Edited by Paul M. Smalley. General Editors Joel R. Beeke and Derek W.H. Thomas. Grand Rapids, Michigan. Reformation Heritage Books. 2015, 44-45.

PERKINS' VIEW OF THE LOCAL CHURCH

Perkins believed the invisible Church was the chosen of God brought to Christ. Regeneration and conversion came only by God's Spirit through the means of the Gospel. Perkins was a staunch promoter of the doctrine of predestination as the identification of the Christian as part of the Church. He writes:

> *"God gives His Holy Spirit to His elect only, who in God's appointed time makes His habitation in them, who does also sweep the floors of their spirits with the hand of His grace and the beesome of His Word and trims up the houses of their hearts with the sweet and pleasant flowers of His Spirit and adorns them with the costly tapestry and precious ornaments of His orient and excellent graces."* [6]

This informed Perkins' understanding of the invisible Church. The people were simply the chosen of God. They were God's sheep who would be brought into God's fold through the means of the Gospel being proclaimed and thereby would profess the true faith in a visible local church that preached a true Gospel.

The local church

Now before we examine Perkins' view of the local church, we must acknowledge that our view of the local church will flow out of our view of the universal, visible Church. Perkins saw the Church invisible as the elect of God. He perceived from Scripture that the universal visible Church was the professors of the faith in the world. Therefore, the local church for Perkins would be those who professed such things as consistent to the kingdom of God, namely its King, its Instructions, and what it meant to be a citizen (one who professed the faith given by the apostles with Christ as the cornerstone). Perkins writes in his exposition on the Sermon on the Mount, "That to believe and confess the doctrine of salvation, taught and delivered by the prophets and apostles, is an infallible

---

6. Perkins, William. *The Manner and Order of Predestination.* Vol. 6 of *The Works of William Perkins.* Edited by Joel R. Beeke and Greg A. Salazar. General Editors Joel R. Beeke and Derek W.H. Thomas. Grand Rapids, Michigan. Reformation Heritage Books. 2018, 156.

and inseparable note of a true church of God."[7] He was clear in his exposition on the Sermon on the Mount that a true particular church, as a representation of the visible church in a geographical location, was to be made up of those who confess the doctrine of salvation. He even went on to say that such a profession of the true way of salvation was an "infallible and inseparable note of a true church of God," which conveys what he believed was central to identifying a true particular church. The profession of the true Gospel was the main mark of a true particular church, according to Perkins' thinking. Perkins was clear on the type of faith that those who made up the church are to profess to have. He writes, "Saving (commonly called justifying) faith, which is a special persuasion wrought by the Holy Ghost in the heart of those that are effectually called concerning their reconciliation and salvation by Christ...."[8] Perkins viewed the Gospel as central to the life of the local church. We read of the Gospel's necessity in the local church, in his statement, "As for the gospel, I take it for that part of the Word of God which promises righteousness and everlasting life to all who believe in Christ, and withal commands this faith."[9] The Gospel preached was the means for men and women to come out of darkness into the spiritual life eternal. Logically it must be seen that Perkins rightly saw the Gospel's centrality and the necessity of its existence in a group of people for them to lay claim to the title of a true church.

Building on the reality that a true church was a group of professors of the biblical Gospel, Perkins would outline what he

---

7. Perkins, William. *Sermon on the Mount: Matthew 5-7. Vol. 1 of The Works of William Perkins.* Edited by J. Stephen Yuille. General Editors Joel R. Beeke and Derek W.H. Thomas. Grand Rapids, Michigan. Reformation Heritage Books. 2014, 310.

8. Perkins, William. *Commentary on Hebrews 11. Vol. 3 of The Works of William Perkins.* Edited by Randall J. Pederson and Ryan Hurd. General Editors Joel R. Beeke and Derek W.H. Thomas. Grand Rapids, Michigan. Reformation Heritage Books. 2017, 6.

9. Perkins, William. *Discourse on Conscience. Vol. 8 of The Works of William Perkins.* Edited by J. Stephen Yuille. General Editors Joel R. Beeke and Derek W.H. Thomas. Grand Rapids, Michigan. Reformation Heritage Books. 2019, 18.

believed would produce such a result, which for him was namely three things: (1) preaching of the Gospel, (2) the administration of the sacraments, and (3) church discipline. Perkins writes in his exposition on the Apostles' Creed:

> "And hence it follows necessarily that the preaching of the doctrine of the prophets and apostles, joined with any measure of faith and obedience, is an infallible mark of a true church. Indeed, it is true, there be three things required to the good estate of the church: the preaching of the gospel, the administration of the sacraments, and the due execution of discipline according to the Word. Yet if the two latter be wanting, so be it there be preaching of the word with obedience in the people, there is for substance a true church of God." [10]

Perkins did acknowledge that a substance of a true local church (a group of sheep, small or large) would still be present if sacraments were not practiced rightly and church discipline was neglected. The one non-negotiable was that the Gospel is rightly preached. Perkins' view here is well thought out and realistic with regard to the time he lived as well as his position within the Church of England. He acknowledged that Christians could exist in unhealthy places as long as the Gospel is there. Yet Perkins hints that unhealthy practices in local churches will engender more goats in the church house that will harm the sheep. Yet the sheep will still exist in a place that preaches the Gospel. Perkins' view of the three marks that make a true local church present is something Owen, who appears to have been influenced by some of Perkins' ideas here, would later convey. In his book, *True Nature of a Gospel Church*, he outlined the requirements for a person to be a member of a local biblical church. Owen used the following terms to define who is received into membership in the local church according to his understanding of Scripture:

---

10. Perkins, William. *Exposition of the Creed. Vol. 5 of The Works of William Perkins*. Edited by Ryan Hurd. General Editors Joel R. Beeke and Derek W.H. Thomas. Grand Rapids, Michigan. Reformation Heritage Books. 2017, 378.

> "They must be such as do make an open profession of the subjection of their souls and consciences unto the authority of Christ in the gospel, and their readiness to yield obedience unto all his commands." [11]

John Owen, in this statement, conveyed the importance of a church membership that made a profession of faith in the Christ of the biblical Gospel and that willfully submitted to Christ in the local church and lived out the faith in public and private. He also believed that children were brought into the visible church under their parents' covenant and were to be baptized as such. [12] For Owen, a person who failed to live up to the membership requirements of said local church was to be rebuked and, if he remained unrepentant, removed from the membership of the church. This shows Owen's high view of who could take of the sacraments and his admonition to perform church discipline. Owen also writes:

> "1. That if there be no more required of any, as unto personal Qualifications, in a visible, uncontrollable profession, to constitute them subjects of Christ's kingdom and members of his church, Ezek. 22:26, but what is required by the most righteous and severe laws of men to constitute a good subject or Citizen, the Distinction between his visible kingdom and the kingdoms of the world, as unto the principal causes of it, is utterly lost. Now, all negative Qualifications, as, that men are not oppressors, drunkards, revilers, swearers, adulterers, etc., are required hereunto; but yet it is so fallen out that generally more is required to constitute such a citizen as shall represent the righteous laws he liveth under than to constitute a member of the church of Christ. 2. That whereas regeneration is expressly required in the gospel to give a right and privilege unto an entrance into the church or kingdom of Christ, John 3:3, Tit. 3:3–5, whereby that kingdom

---

11. Owen, John. *True Nature of a Gospel Church*. Vol. 16. of *The Works of John Owen*. (ed. William H. Goold. London: The Banner of Truth Trust. 1981), 14.

12. Owen, John. *True Nature of a Gospel Church*. Vol. 16. of *The Works of John Owen*. (ed. William H. Goold. London: The Banner of Truth Trust. 1981), 22.

> of his is distinguished from all other kingdoms in and of the world, unto an interest wherein never any such thing was required, it must of necessity be something better, more excellent and sublime, than anything the laws and policies of men pretend unto or prescribe. Wherefore it cannot consist in any outward rite, easy to be observed by the worst and vilest of men. Besides, the Scripture gives us a description of it in opposition unto its consisting in any such rite, 1 Pet. 3:21; and many things required unto good citizens are far better than the mere observation of such a rite. 3. Of this regeneration baptism is the symbol, the sign, the expression, and representation, John 3:5; Acts 2:38; 1 Pet. 3:21. Wherefore, unto those who are in a due manner partakers of it, it giveth all the external rights and privileges which belong unto them that are regenerate, until they come unto such seasons wherein the personal performance of those duties whereon the continuation of the estate of visible regeneration doth depend is required of them. Herein if they fail, they lose all privilege and benefit by their baptism.
>
> "God alone is judge concerning this regeneration, as unto its internal, real principle and state in the souls of men, Acts 15:8, Rev. 2:23, whereon the participation of all the spiritual advantages of the covenant of grace doth depend. The church is judge of its evidences and fruits in their external demonstration, as unto a participation of the outward privileges of a regenerate state, and no farther, Acts 8:13. And we shall hereon briefly declare what belongs unto the forming of a right judgment herein, and who are to be esteemed fit members of any gospel church-state, or have a right so to be." [13]

Owen is clear that in the local church, no one can judge for certain a person's regeneration. Rather, the church is to assess the evidence of such professors with charity under the covenant of grace. Owen anticipated that the local church would have both tares and wheat. He also writes:

---

13. Owen, John. *True Nature of a Gospel Church*. Vol. 16. of *The Works of John Owen*. (ed. William H. Goold. London: The Banner of Truth Trust. 1981), 12-13.

> "In this division, let there be, in the name of Christ, and the fear of God, a gathering of professors (visible saints, men and women of good knowledge and upright conversation, -so holding forth their communion with Christ), by their own desire and voluntary consent, into one body,—uniting themselves, by virtue of some promissory engagement or otherwise, to perform all mutual duties, to walk in love and peace, spiritual and church communion, as beseemeth the gospel." [14]

Owen had a clear view of a visible church being made up of those who profess allegiance to Christ Jesus as revealed in the Gospel as seen in his phrase above "their own desire and voluntary consent, into one body, -uniting themselves by virtue of some promissory engagement or otherwise, to perform all mutual duties." [15] Owen developed the ideas we read in Perkins with regard to what a member is and further clarified what church membership should be and look like. Perkins' thought is replete in Owen's statement above and hints at the kingdom ideology in the wording Owen uses. The following statement by Owen concerning the local church conveys the concepts of a King, the Word as instruction, and who the citizens are:

> "In **the name of Christ**, and the fear of God, **a gathering of professors** (visible saints, men and women of good knowledge and upright conversation, -so holding forth their communion with Christ), by their own desire and voluntary consent, into one body,—uniting themselves, by virtue of some promissory engagement or otherwise, **to perform all mutual duties**." [16]

The local church, per Perkins and Owen after him, was a visible group of professors. Such a group professed Jesus as King and head

---

14. Owen, John. *Sermons. A Country Essay: For the Practice of Church Government*. Vol. 8. of *The Works of John Owen*. (ed. William H. Goold. London: The Banner of Truth Trust. 1982), 51.

15. Ibid., 51.

16. Owen, John. *Sermons. A Country Essay: For the Practice of Church Government*. Vol. 8. of *The Works of John Owen*. (ed. William H. Goold. London: The Banner of Truth Trust. 1982), 51. (Emphasis mine)

of the church, to be themselves governed by the Word in their life and worship of God, and as professors, those who were to keep each other accountable in their profession of faith.

The imperative of the worship of God in the local church

Having outlined Perkins' view of the local church, we must ask how he viewed the services of such a gathering in the local church. Did he adhere to a normative principle of worship? We understand the normative principle of worship to assert that if the Word of God does not expressly forbid an element or practice of worship, then it is acceptable, as Luther and others taught. Or did Perkins hold to the regulative principle of worship, requiring an explicit scriptural command in order for an element or practice to be used in the worship of the church? In order to grasp Perkins' thought, we must understand that his commitment was to worship God only by the Word of God. He writes in *A Warning Against the Idolatry of Last Times*:

> "Nothing may go under the name of the worship of God, which He has not ordained in His own Word and commanded to us as His own worship (Deut. 12:8, 32). For we are forbidden under pain of the curse of God, either to add or take away anything from the precepts of God in which He prescribes His own worship. When the Jews worshipped God after the devised fashions of the Gentiles, though their meaning was to worship God, yet the text says, 'they worshipped nothing but devils' (Deut. 32:17). Again, the Lord forbids us in His worship to follow 'after our own hearts and eyes' (Num. 15:39)." [17]

Perkins saw anything done in the service regarding the elements of worship that were not prescribed or described in the

---

17. Perkins, William. *A Warning Against the Idolatry of Last Times.* Vol. 7 of *The Works of William Perkins.* Edited by Shawn D. Wright and Andrew S. Ballitch. General Editors Joel R. Beeke and Derek W.H. Thomas. Grand Rapids, Michigan. Reformation Heritage Books. 2019, 477.

Word of God as something to be avoided. Not only was it to be avoided, but it was also forbidden to do as he conveys in his statement above: "For we are forbidden under pain of the curse of God, either to add or take away anything from the precepts of God in which He prescribes His own worship." "Perkins was committed to something similar to what is now called 'the regulative principle,' especially with regards to the elements of worship, but he also maintained that governance and maintenance of the church visible may be ordered in divers times in different ways." He would have seen the normative principle as held by many in the time of this writing as too loose, unhelpful, and leading to impurity in the worship of the Triune God. In this statement, we can perceive that Perkins was analyzing the elements passed down to be carried out in the worship gathering, thinking through what Roman church elements were justifiable according to Scripture admonition or inference. Much of what happens in Protestantism in our time would likely come under fire from men like Perkins, who would see the practices of instantaneous baptism, dances, extemporaneous outbursts of supposed giftings, skits, concert-like performances, etc., all as a violation of Scripture and an aberration of God's praise in the gathering of God's people to worship the Triune God. God's worship must be according to His Word and carried out in an orderly manner (1 Corinthians 14:40).

What about the Lord's Day as the Christian Sabbath?

When was the local church to gather? When were they to meet? Perkins would break away from Calvin's view, though Calvin seemed to be a practicing Sabbatarian, to a more robust understanding of the Lord's Day being the day the church gathered as a Christian Sabbath. Perkins appealed to Scripture to support his claims, as we will see. He posited the question in his writings, "Is the Sabbath day still valid?" First, we need to see the view he broke away from. According to a book review written by Tony Lane, where Calvin's view is analyzed, he writes, "Calvin rejects the view that the moral part of the commandment is the fixing of one day in seven, while the ceremonial part (which particular day) has been changed."[18] Calvin, in his *Institutes*, writes:

> *"If superstition is dreaded, there was more danger in keeping the Jewish Sabbath than the Lord's day as Christians now do. It being expedient to overthrow superstition, the Jewish holy day was abolished; and as a thing necessary to retain decency, order, and peace in the church, another day was appointed for that purpose. It was not, however, without a reason that the early Christians substituted what we call the Lord's Day for the Sabbath . . . But this is nothing else than to insult the Jews, by changing the day, and yet mentally attributing to it the same sanctity; thus retaining the same typical distinction of days as had place among the Jews. And of a truth, we see what profit they had made by such doctrine. Those who cling to their constitutions go thrice as far as the Jews in the gross and carnal superstition of sabbatism; so that the rebukes which we read in Isaiah (Isaiah 1:13; 58:13) apply as much to those of the present day, as to those to whom the prophet addressed them. We must be careful, however, to observe the general doctrine, i.e., in order that religion may neither be lost nor languish amongst us, we must diligently attend on our religious assemblies, and duly avail ourselves of those external aids which tend to promote the worship of God."* [19]

Lane's statement seems substantiated in light of Calvin's teaching in the *Institutes*. Calvin held that the Lord's Day was necessary for order in the church but was not the Christian Sabbath (as would later be expounded by the Westminster Confession of Faith and the Second London Baptist 1689 Confession). Calvin taught the Lord's Day was necessary for churches as a day to gather but was not the New Testament version of the Sabbath day rooted in Creation and in the Moral Law. He did not hold the Sabbath principle as part of the law that carried forward into New

---

18. Lane, Tony. *Review of Calvin and the Sabbath* by Richard Gaffin. Themelios, Volume 25. Issue 3.

19. Calvin, John. *Institutes of the Christian Religion*. Translated by Henry Beveridge. Peabody, Massachusetts. Hendrickson. 2008, 253.

Testament times, but likely as a type fulfilled in the antitype of Christ. Perkins' thought appears to have broken off from Calvin on this issue. Perkins argued in his work on Revelation 1-3 that the Sabbath day being the Lord's Day was not the result of Christian emperors or pronouncements made by those in authority. He argues that the Sabbath day being on Sunday in the New Covenant, finds its basis in Scripture first and foremost.[20] Perkins writes in *Digest or Harmony of the Books of the Old and New Testament*:

> "The Sabbath of the new world is the day of Christ's resurrection, which is the eighth day from creation: and I think that the Scripture seems to assign the Sabbath to the Lord's day (1 Corinthians 16:1). To make gathering on the first day of the week is an apostolic institution, therefore the hallowing of this day for the Sabbath is likewise an apostolic institution, because gatherings were not made but when the worship of God was solemnly performed. Secondly, John the apostle does acknowledge this day to be the Lord's (Revelation 1:10), that is, a day consecrated to the honor of Christ. And the rest of the apostles have observed this same day instead of the Jews' Sabbath (Acts 20:7). Yes, Christ Himself does seem to have done the same (John 20:19, 26). Thirdly, it is the opinion of Cyprian, that circumcision was a sacrament of the Sabbath to be kept on the eighth day in the New Testament. 'The Lord's Day' was hallowed by Christ's resurrection.'"[21]

Perkins clearly outlined the Lord's Day as the Sabbath. For example, in the above quotation, he states: "The Sabbath of the new world is the day of Christ's resurrection," "I think that the Scripture seems to assign the Sabbath to the Lord's Day,"

---

20. Perkins' argument for the Lord Jesus being the author of this change of Sabbath day, not the church, is found in: Perkins, William. *Exposition of Revelation 1-3*. Vol. 4 of *The Works of William Perkins*. Edited by J. Stephen Yuille. General Editors Joel R. Beeke and Derek W.H. Thomas. Grand Rapids, Michigan. Reformation Heritage Books. 2017, 370-375.

21. Perkins, William. *Digest or Harmony of the Old and New Testaments*. Vol. 1 of *The Works of William Perkins*. Edited by J. Stephen Yuille. General Editors Joel R. Beeke and Derek W.H. Thomas. Grand Rapids, Michigan. Reformation Heritage Books. 2014, 19-20.

"therefore hallowing of this day for the Sabbath." [22] Perkins' break from Calvin's view is not a light matter in principle. This view of the Christian Sabbath today is not as widely held as it once was in the days of the Puritans. Rather than using Calvin and others as justification, many in Protestantism treat the day as any other. Perhaps reading Perkins' view would stir us to reconsider in wider Protestantism the practice of the Lord's Day as the Christian's Sabbath and how God designed it to benefit us.

What was required of professors to be part of the local church?

Thus far, we have uncovered Perkins' view of the local church. We have seen the three marks of a true local church as well as the centrality of the Gospel and the day the local church was to gather according to Perkins' exposition of the Scripture. Now we must ask practically how a church was to discern who its members should be. How was membership handled? Perkins, being a very practical Puritan, writes concerning the church's responsibility to their members in his work on the Apostles' Creed. He states:

> "But to proceed, how are the members of the visible church qualified and discerned? The answer follows in the definition, 'professing the faith.' Whereby I mean the profession of that religion which has been taught from the beginning and is now recorded in the writings of the prophets and apostles. And this profession is a sign and mark whereby a man is declared and made manifest to be a member of the church. Again, because the profession of the faith is otherwhiles true and sincere and otherwiles only in show, therefore there be also two sorts of members of the visible church: members before God and members before men. A member of the church before God is he that besides the outward profession of the faith has inwardly a pure heart, good conscience, and faith unfeigned, whereby he is indeed a true member of the church. Members before men, whom we may call reputed members, are such as have nothing

22. Ibid., 19-20.

else but the outward profession, wanting the good conscience and the faith unfeigned. The reason why they are to be esteemed members of us is because we are bound by the rule of charity to think of men as they appear unto us, leaving secret judgment to God." [23]

Perkins posited that those who professed the apostolic faith were allowed to join, yet he believed that only God knew the true condition of each member. He categorizes members into "members before God" and "members before men." The first category was those whose outward profession came from a true inward sincerity, whereas those who were "members before men" may have professed the doctrine of faith outwardly but lacked the inward heart purified by faith. What Perkins is acknowledging is the limitation that any local church has. According to Perkins, they are bound by charity to receive members based on the profession of the doctrines of the faith. Yet he acknowledges that there will be those who come into the membership who are not truly members of the elect of God but are tares among the wheat. This is telling of Perkins' understanding of the reality of ministering in a fallen world. It did not deter him from his striving to see a biblically faithful local church. Yet he knew there would be those who would confess the doctrines of faith before men yet, in time, prove to be false professors. This ideology can be seen in John Owen's later works. Owen, as one of the greatest theologians of the Puritan era, would write in greater detail than Perkins concerning church membership. In his book, *True Nature of a Gospel Church*, John Owen defined what he believed membership should entail within a local church. John Owen wrote:

> *"In this division, let there be, in the name of Christ, and the fear of God, a gathering of professors (visible saints, men and women of good knowledge and upright conversation, -so holding forth their communion with Christ), by their own desire and voluntary consent, into one*

---

[23]. Perkins, William. *Exposition of the Creed. Vol. 5 of The Works of William Perkins.* Edited by Ryan Hurd. General Editors Joel R. Beeke and Derek W.H. Thomas. Grand Rapids, Michigan. Reformation Heritage Books. 2017, 377.

PERKINS' VIEW OF THE LOCAL CHURCH

body,—uniting themselves, by virtue of some promissory engagement or otherwise, to perform all mutual duties, to walk in love and peace, spiritual and church communion, as beseemeth the gospel." [24]

What is fascinating here about Owen's thought is that it mimics much of Perkins' thought yet further expounds the terms and emphasizes the covenant unto the children of believers. Perkins' thought seems to be one of the influences that the later Puritans, like Owen, developed to outline biblical procedures for the local church's membership with greater focus and precision.

Perkins was clear that members of the invisible Church alone (the elect of God) were the recipients of salvation by faith in Christ. He believed the exclusive Gospel produced a people exclusively for God. He writes about the necessity of knowing Christ to be saved:

> *"For very few there are who know Him as they ought. The Turk, even at this very day, knows Him not but as He was a prophet. The Jew scorns His cross and passion. The popish churches, though in word they confess Him, yet they do not know Him as they ought. The friars and Jesuits in their sermons at this day commonly use the passion as a means to stir up pity and compassion toward Christ who, being so righteous a man, was so hardly intreated, and to inflame their hearers to a hatred of the Jews, and Judas, and Pontius Pilate, who put our blessed Savior to death. But all this may be done in any other history. And the service of God, which in that church stands now in force by the canons of the Council of Trent, defaces Christ crucified, in that the passions of martyrs are made meritorious, the very wood of the cross their only help, and the virgin Mary the 'queen of heaven' and a 'mother of mercy,' who in remission of sins may command her Son. And they give religious adoration to dumb crucifixes made by the hand and art of man."* [25]

---

24. Owen, John. *Sermons. A Country Essay: For the Practice of Church Government*. Vol. 8. of *The Works of John Owen*. (ed. William H. Goold. London: The Banner of Truth Trust. 1982), 51.

25. Perkins, William. *True Manner of Knowing Christ Crucified*. Vol. 9 of *The Works of William Perkins*. Edited by J. Stephen Yuille. General Editors Joel R. Beeke and Derek W.H. Thomas. Grand Rapids, Michigan. Reformation

Perkins clearly saw the Roman church as having strayed from the foundation of the apostolic Gospel, whereby men and women would be saved. Therefore, the invisible Church would have few of its members in such an institution. Remember from earlier that Perkins' view of the invisible Church can be summarized as God's elect drawn to Him by the true Gospel in this time and ultimately in all time. He saw the local church as a manifestation of the universal catholic visible Church in a geographical area under biblical government. There is much to learn from Perkins' understanding of the church from Scripture, and much the Protestant church needs to rediscover concerning his three marks of a true church, namely: Gospel preaching, proper administration of the sacraments, and the practice of church discipline.

Conclusion

William Perkins' view of the local church and the Lord's Day as the Christian Sabbath is thoroughly rooted in scriptural precepts, principles, and examples. His view of the invisible Church being the elect of God in Christ is rooted in the ideology we read in Scripture, such as Ephesians 1:3-6 which states:

> *"Blessed be the God and Father of our Lord Jesus Christ, who has blessed us in Christ with every spiritual blessing in the heavenly places, even as he chose us in him before the foundation of the world, that we should be holy and blameless before him. In love he predestined us for adoption to himself as sons through Jesus Christ, according to the purpose of his will, to the praise of his glorious grace, with which he has blessed us in the Beloved."*

The elect of God the Father given to Christ Jesus the Son (John 10:27-30) as a reward for His suffering is the invisible Church from all time, and Perkins wholeheartedly upheld this view. As quoted earlier, he writes:

Heritage Books. 2020, 16-17.

PERKINS' VIEW OF THE LOCAL CHURCH

> *"God gives His Holy Spirit to His elect only, who in God's appointed time makes His habitation in them, who does also sweep the floors of their spirits with the hand of His grace and the beesome of His Word and trims up the houses of their hearts with the sweet and pleasant flowers of His Spirit and adorns them with the costly tapestry and precious ornaments of His orient and excellent graces."* [26]

We see in this his usage of the elect as those who receive the Holy Spirit. The justification of such a statement is likely found in texts like Ephesians 1:3-14, whereby the true people of God are outlined and described. Perkins connects the identity of the invisible Church to the doctrine of election. He ties election to being indwelt by the Spirit of God, which is the outcome in time and space of the predestination of God concerning such a people. In a review of his understanding of the invisible Church, Perkins' perspective is thoroughly rooted in his understanding of God's sovereignty over history and salvation, in contrast to the popish view in Roman Catholic theology that he ardently wrote against.

With the church visible (both in the world and locally), Perkins uses the imagery of a King, citizens, and precepts. He rightly explains that the local church is the church visible in a region under a prescribed church government. In outlining his view, he has sympathy toward a Presbyterian-type ideology of government, though he never left the English church. He believed that those admitted into the local church must have a profession of faith, but no one could determine their regeneration with full assurance; therefore, charity must be given. John Owen wrote:

> *"They must be such as do make an open profession of the subjection of their souls and consciences unto the authority of Christ in the gospel, and their readiness to yield obedience unto all his commands."* [27]

---

26. Perkins, William. *The Manner and Order of Predestination.* Vol. 6 of *The Works of William Perkins.* Edited by Joel R. Beeke and Greg A. Salazar. General Editors Joel R. Beeke and Derek W.H. Thomas. Grand Rapids, Michigan. Reformation Heritage Books. 2018, 291.

27. Owen, John. *True Nature of a Gospel Church.* Vol. 16. of *The Works of John Owen.* (ed. William H. Goold. London: The Banner of Truth Trust. 1981), 14.

With regard to his view of the Christian Sabbath, Perkins' driving thought was the Moral Law and the Sabbath as part of that. His upholding of the Ten Commandments as the Moral Law guides his analysis of the Sabbath and his refutation of the ideology that Calvin proposed. Perkins writes:

> "The Sabbath of the new world is the day of Christ's resurrection, which is the eighth day from creation: and I think that the Scripture seems to assign the Sabbath to the Lord's day (1 Corinthians 16:1). To make gathering on the first day of the week is an apostolic institution, therefore the hallowing of this day for the Sabbath is likewise an apostolic institution, because gatherings were not made but when the worship of God was solemnly performed. Secondly, John the apostle does acknowledge this day to be the Lord's (Revelation 1:10), that is, a day consecrated to the honor of Christ. And the rest of the apostles have observed this same day instead of the Jews' Sabbath (Acts 20:7). Yes, Christ Himself does seem to have done the same (John 20:19, 26). Thirdly, it is the opinion of Cyprian, that circumcision was a sacrament of the Sabbath to be kept on the eight day in the New Testament. 'The Lord's Day was hallowed by Christ's resurrection.'"[28]

His usage of Revelation 1:10, as well as his conclusion that the New Testament seems to assign the Sabbath Day to the day the Lord Jesus rose from the dead, is well supported by Scripture and inference from Scripture. His argument was convincing, and in this case, Calvin's argument, less so. Overall, Perkins' theology of the church is scriptural, clear, concise, and potent.

---

28. Perkins, William. *Digest or Harmony of the Old and New Testaments. Vol. 1 of The Works of William Perkins.* Edited by J. Stephen Yuille. General Editors Joel R. Beeke and Derek W.H. Thomas. Grand Rapids, Michigan. Reformation Heritage Books. 2014, 19-20.

Chapter Three

INTRODUCTION TO PERKINS' VIEW OF THE SACRAMENTS

THERE IS MUCH CONFUSION in the area of the sacraments today in the Protestant church. The London Baptist Confession of 1689 calls baptism and the Lord's Supper "ordinances." The Confession states: "1. Baptism and the Lord's Supper are ordinances of positive and sovereign institution. They are appointed by the Lord Jesus the only lawgiver and are to be continued in his church to the end of the age."[1] The London Baptist Confession, which was the Baptist version of the Westminster truths, is careful not to assert that grace has been conveyed in baptism and the Lord's Supper. The London Baptist Confession called the two sacraments of the church *ordinances* as it expressed the view that baptism and the Lord's Supper are God-ordained ceremonies to be adhered to in the local church. Calvin and Perkins would want to go further than such language.

What is a sacrament, and what are the sacraments in the church today? Calvin taught what the sacraments are in his *Institutes*. He writes much on the topic, but in section 1 and section 20 on this topic, he outlines it with great clarity. Calvin writes:

---

1. The 1689 Baptist Confession of Faith. Chapter 28—Baptism and the Lord's Supper—Founders. Section 1. Ministries.https://founders.org/library/chapter-28-baptism-and-the-lords-supper/.

"1. Akin to the preaching of the gospel, we have another help to our faith in the sacraments, in regard to which, it greatly concerns us that some sure doctrine should be delivered, informing us both of the end for which they were instituted, and of their present use. First, we must attend to what a sacrament is. It seems to me, then, a simple and appropriate definition to say, that it is an external sign, by which the Lord seals on our consciences his promises of good-will toward us, in order to sustain the weakness of our faith, and we in our turn testify our piety towards him, both before himself, and before angels as well as men. We may also define more briefly by calling it a testimony of the divine favour toward us, confirmed by an external sign, with a corresponding attestation of our faith towards Him. You may make your choice of these definitions, which in meaning differ not from that of Augustine, which defines a sacrament to be a visible sign of a sacred thing, or a visible form of an invisible grace, but does not contain a better or surer explanation. As its brevity makes it somewhat obscure, and thereby misleads the more illiterate, I wished to remove all doubt, and make the definition fuller by stating it at greater length. 20. Now these have been different at different times, according to the dispensation which the Lord has seen meet to employ in manifesting himself to men. Circumcision was enjoined on Abraham and his posterity, and to it were afterwards added purifications and sacrifices, and other rites of the Mosaic Law. These were the sacraments of the Jews even until the advent of Christ. After these were abrogated, the two sacraments of Baptism and the Lord's Supper, which the Christian Church now employs, were instituted." [2]

Calvin held that the sacraments were a sign which sealed the promises of God to the conscience of the people of God to sustain them in their weakness in faith. It was a visible sign of an invisible grace, as he describes it. This phrasing makes it clear that he believed it was more than a symbolic remembrance. He conveyed in

2. Calvin, John. *Institutes of the Christian Religion.* Translated by Henry Beveridge. John Calvin: Institutes of the Christian Religion—Christian Classics Ethereal Library (ccel.org). Chapter 14. Section 1, 20.

INTRODUCTION TO PERKINS' VIEW OF THE SACRAMENTS

section 20 that the sacraments were baptism and the Lord's Supper, perhaps though the clearest exposition of the doctrine of the sacraments comes from the Westminster Confession of Faith.

The Westminster Confession of Faith was constructed within the same century of Perkins' last years of life by faithful men who sought to present the doctrines of Scripture to the English people and government as called upon by Parliament. They drew up in the year 1646 a comprehensive statement of faith. In the Westminster Confession of Faith, Chapter 27: "Of the Sacraments" defined the sacraments as:

> "1. Sacraments are holy signs and seals of the covenant of grace, immediately instituted by God, to represent Christ and his benefits, and to confirm our interest in him: as also to put a visible difference between those that belong unto the Church and the rest of the world; and solemnly to engage them to the service of God in Christ, according to his Word. 2. There is in every sacrament a spiritual relation or sacramental union, between the sign and the thing signified; whence it comes to pass that the names and the effects of the one are attributed to the other. 4. There be only two sacraments ordained by Christ our Lord in the Gospel, that is to say, Baptism and the Supper of the Lord: neither of which may be dispensed by any but by a minister of the Word lawfully ordained."[3]

The view of the sacraments the Westminster divines took was they were holy signs and seals of the covenant of grace, that each sacrament contains a union between the sign and the thing signified. The only two sacraments of the New Testament are baptism and the Lord's Supper.

Perkins would have heartily consented to the language the Westminster divines used. He defined *sacrament* in his work, *The Foundation of the Christian Religion*: "A sign to represent, a seal to confirm, an instrument to convey Christ and all His benefits to them that do believe in Him (Genesis 17:11; Romans 4:11;

---

3. Westminster Confession of Faith. Chapter 27: Of the Sacraments. Section 1, 2, and 4.

Galatians 3:1)."[4] He used the "sign and seal" language here as well as connecting it to the benefits of Christ given to those who believe on Christ, showing faith is required to receive the sacrament. William Perkins writes in his great work entitled *Golden Chain*:

> "A sacrament is that whereby Christ and His saving graces are by external rites signified, exhibited, and sealed to a Christian man . . . God alone is the author of a sacrament, for the sign cannot confirm anything at all but by the consent and promise of him at whose hands the benefit promise must be received."[5]

He goes on to write: "The parts of a sacrament are the sign and the thing of the sacrament. The sign is either the matter sensible or the action conversant about the same."[6] William Perkins' position on the sacraments and what the sacraments were in the church is further outlined in *Golden Chain*:

> "There are two sacraments . . . The first sacrament is that whereby Christians are initiated and admitted into the church of God, and this is baptism. The second sacrament, whereby they are perpetually preserved and nourished in the same church, is the Lord's Supper."[7]

Perkins, with clarity, outlined, as Calvin did before him, the sacraments of the church being both baptism and the Lord's Supper. He denied them as mere symbolic representations, which is a popular view held today in many Protestant and evangelical churches. Rather, Perkins conveyed what the Westminster divines codified for the church just years after his death.

---

4. Perkins, William. *The Foundation of Christian Religion.* Vol. 5 of *The Works of William Perkins.* Edited by Ryan Hurd. General Editors Joel R. Beeke and Derek W.H. Thomas. Grand Rapids, Michigan. Reformation Heritage Books. 2017, 505.

5. Perkins, William. *Golden Chain.* Vol. 6 of *The Works of William Perkins.* Edited by Joel R. Beeke and Greg A. Salazar. General Editors Joel R. Beeke and Derek W.H. Thomas. Grand Rapids, Michigan. Reformation Heritage Books. 2018, 156.

6. Ibid., 157.

7. Ibid, 161.

INTRODUCTION TO PERKINS' VIEW OF THE SACRAMENTS

Proper use of sacraments

William Perkins sought to define the sacraments and analyze their proper use. In his writings on this issue, he had much pastoral sensitivity to the reality that not all who partake of the sacraments are in the proper position to do so. Perkins writes about the three categories of people who receive the sacrament:

> "The holy use of the sacrament is when such as are truly converted do use those rites which God has prescribed to the true ends of the sacrament. Therefore, (1) the reprobate, though God offer the whole sacrament to them, yet they receive the signs alone without the things signified by the signs, because the sign without the right use thereof is not a sacrament to the receiver of it ... (2) The elect as yet not converted to the Lord do receive in like manner the bare signs without the thing signified, yet so as the sacrament shall in them afterward have its good affect. For the sacrament received before a man's conversion is afterward to the penitent both ratified and becomes profitable; and that use of the sacrament which before was utterly unlawful does then become very lawful. (3) The elect already converted due to their salvation receive both the sign and the thing signified together, yet so as that for their unworthy receiving thereof, the which comes to pass by reason of their manifold infirmities and relapse into sin, they are subject to temporal punishments."[8]

Perkins made clear that these signs made the invisible grace of God in the promises visible to the believer's senses and eyes. The grace of God in Christ was made visible to the senses to the believer who came to the sacrament by faith in the promises of God that are yes in the Lord Jesus.

He was clear in outlining the purpose of the sacrament and guarded the sacraments in the church. Perkins wanted to answer why the sacraments were given and how they were to be approached. He was not content to just outline what they were but wanted to convey God's intended ordained purpose. Perkins writes:

8. Ibid, 159.

> "The end why a sacrament was ordained is (1) for the better confirmation of our faith, for by it as by certain pledges given God of His great mercy does as it were bind Himself to us. Now a sacrament does confirm our faith not by any inherent or proper power it has in itself, as has a sovereign medicine received by a patient, the which, whether a man sleep or wake, confirms his strength; but rather by reasoning and using the signs when the Holy Ghost shall frame in our hearts such a conclusion, as this: All such as are converted, rightly using the sacraments, shall receive Christ and His graces . . . (2) That it may be a badge and note of that profession by which the true church of God is distinguished from other congregations. (3) That it might be a means to preserve and spread abroad the doctrine of the gospel. (4) It serves to bind the faithful that they do continue both loyal and grateful to their Lord God. (5) it is the bond of mutual amity between the faithful." [9]

He went on to write on the many differences between the Old Testament sacraments and the New Testament sacraments:

> "(1) They were many; these but few. (2) They pointed at Christ to come; these show that He is come. (3) They were appropriate to the posterity of Abraham, but these are common to the whole church called out of the Jews and Gentiles." [10]

Perkins argues for what is now the Westminster position of the sacraments from these brief sections of his writings. He emphasized their importance in binding the faithful in their loyalty to Christ Jesus the King as they received Christ through the sacraments in His graces to strengthen their faith. Acutely aware of the Romish error, he was clear and firm in the limitations of the sacrament. He made it abundantly clear that the sacraments were not a sign that grants justifying grace. He goes on to write to show the sacraments themselves do not save:

---

9. Ibid., 158.
10. Ibid., 159.

INTRODUCTION TO PERKINS' VIEW OF THE SACRAMENTS

> "The covenant of grace is absolutely necessary to salvation; for of necessity a man must be within the covenant and receive Christ Jesus, the very substance thereof, or perish eternally. But a sacrament is not absolutely necessary, but only as it is a prop and stay for faith to lean upon. For it cannot entitle us into the inheritance of the sons of God, as the covenant does, but only by reason of faith going before it does seal that which before was bestowed upon us ... Therefore, the want of a sacrament does not condemn, but the contempt is that which will condemn a man ... The holy use of a sacrament is when such as are truly converted do use those rites which God has prescribed to the true ends of the sacrament."[11]

Notice his phrasing: "A sacrament is not absolutely necessary, but only as it is a prop and stay for faith to lean upon." For Perkins, the sacraments did not grant justification. They strengthened the faith of a believer as a prop strengthens the item it holds up. Perkins was sensitive to what Rome taught and used clear language to contradict their doctrine. Yet he did not downplay the importance of the sacrament, as seen in his statement, "The want of a sacrament does not condemn, but the contempt is that which will condemn a man." He saw the sacraments as to be approached reverently and with humility by faith. Perhaps Paul's admonitions in 1 Corinthians 11:27-28 were in view. The sacraments were clearly upheld and posited by Perkins, sharing in the Reformed tradition from Calvin and his thought seen in the later Westminster Confession. Perkins spent much time working through the ideology of the sacrament as he stood on the shoulders of Calvin and others to refute the error of Rome and convey what the sacrament was and is for God's people. In doing so, he rejected the seven sacraments of Rome and held that the church has two sacraments instituted by the Lord Jesus.

---

11. Ibid., 158-159.

Chapter Four
PERKINS' VIEW OF BAPTISM

WHAT IS BAPTISM? How does it work, and who is to be baptized? These questions, which are asked today, were pondered by the Puritans and their successors. At the forefront, it is helpful to examine baptism from the Scripture and then see how Calvin saw baptism for both of these sources influenced Perkins. The Lord Jesus stated in Matthew 28:16-20:

> "Now the eleven disciples went to Galilee, to the mountain to which Jesus had directed them. And when they saw him they worshiped him, but some doubted. And Jesus came and said to them, 'All authority in heaven and on earth has been given to me. Go therefore and make disciples of all nations, baptizing them in the name of the Father and of the Son and of the Holy Spirit, teaching them to observe all that I have commanded you. And behold, I am with you always, to the end of the age.'"

The apostolic group, as the foundation of the Church with Christ as the cornerstone (Ephesians 2:19-21), was given the Great Commission as part of the foundation of the church to baptize in the name of the Triune God. Instituted by the Lord Jesus for the church, baptism is to be practiced until His return. The Reformers were clear on the importance of baptism. Calvin writes:

"1. Baptism is the initiatory sign by which we are admitted to the fellowship of the Church, that being ingrafted into Christ we may be accounted children of God. Moreover, the end for which God has given it (this I have shown to be common to all mysteries) is, first, that it may be conducive to our faith in him; and, secondly, that it may serve the purpose of a confession among men. The nature of both institutions we shall explain in order. Baptism contributes to our faith three things, which require to be treated separately. The first object, therefore, for which it is appointed by the Lord, is to be a sign and evidence of our purification, or (better to explain my meaning) it is a kind of sealed instrument by which he assures us that all our sins are so deleted, covered, and effaced, that they will never come into his sight, never be mentioned, never imputed. For it is his will that all who have believed, be baptised for the remission of sins. Hence those who have thought that baptism is nothing else than the badge and mark by which we profess our religion before men, in the same way as soldiers attest their profession by bearing the insignia of their commander, having not attended to what was the principal thing in baptism; and this is, that we are to receive it in connection with the promise, 'He that believeth and is baptised shall be saved' (Mark 16:16)." [1]

Calvin, in his *Institutes*, makes clear the Reformed position that baptism is not just an initiation sign into the covenant, but it is not less than an initiation into the visible community. Calvin held that converts to Christianity and the children of one faithful parent were to have the sign applied to them. Perkins did not depart from this understanding of baptism. There would be later Puritan dissenters who would reject the children of believers being baptized, men such as Keach, Kiffin, and others later in the seventeenth century. With regards to baptism William Perkins writes:

"Baptism is a sacrament by which such as are within the covenant are washed with water in the name of the Father,

---

1. Calvin, John. *Institutes of the Christian Religion*. Translated by Henry Beveridge. John Calvin: Institutes of the Christian Religion—Christian Classics Ethereal Library (ccel.org). Chapter 15. Section 1.

> the Son, and the Holy Ghost, that being thus engrafted into Christ they may have perpetual fellowship with Him . . . Within the covenant are all the seeds of Abraham or the seed of the faithful. These are either riper years or infants. Those of riper years are all such as adjoining themselves to the visible church do both testify their repentance of their sins and hold the foundations of religion taught in the same church . . . Infants within the covenant are such as have one at the least of their parents faithful." 2

We read here in this quotation that Perkins was clear that baptism was given to those of riper years who convert or children of one faithful parent. It is a visible sign of the invisible spiritual reality, according to Perkins. Perkins was clear to separate regeneration from the act of baptism though he conveyed baptism signified such a reality to the recipient. Perkins writes, "When shall a man then see the effect of his baptism? At what time soever he does receive Christ by faith, though it is many years after, he shall then feel the power of God to regenerate him and to work all things in him, which He offered in baptism (Hebrews 10:20; 1 Peter 3:20)."[3] Perkins conveys that the power of regeneration which was offered to him in the promises of baptism was not something baptism produced in the person, rather that was the work of God. Perkins viewed that baptism was not salvific when he writes:

> "Such men, whatsoever they be, have indeed the outward baptism of water, but they never received the inward baptism of the Spirit; they wear Christ's livery, but as yet they do service unto Satan; and though they have been made partakers of the seals of the covenant, yet still they abide within the kingdom of darkness; for Christ here teaches by His own example, that all those who have received the

---

2. Perkins, William. *Golden Chain*. Vol. 6 of *The Works of William Perkins*. Edited by Joel R. Beeke and Greg A. Salazar. General Editors Joel R. Beeke and Derek W.H. Thomas. Grand Rapids, Michigan. Reformation Heritage Books. 2018, 161-162.

3. Perkins, William. *The Foundation of Christian Religion*. Vol. 5 of *The Works of William Perkins*. Edited by Ryan Hurd. General Editors Joel R. Beeke and Derek W.H. Thomas. Grand Rapids, Michigan. Reformation Heritage Books. 2017, 506.

inward baptism of the Spirit, whereby they have effectually put off sin, and put on the Lord Jesus, are as sure to be tempted by Satan as Himself was." [4]

He writes *here of the possibility of having the outward sign without the inward reality.* (Emphasis mine) He makes it clear that those who have been baptized in the Spirit are not always those who have been baptized with water. Perkins' logic was simply that the sign does not always mean that the one who received it will experience the reality of what the sacrament signified. It is entirely possible for a man and his family to have received the sacrament without the reality of what it conveys having been manifested in their inner person. By using such logic, Perkins makes clear his position that baptism is not salvific, as Rome taught. It does not impart justifying grace. According to the Catholic Catechism, which summarizes Catholic dogma, baptism is a justifying sacrament. Section 1227 states, "The baptized have 'put on Christ.' Through the Holy Spirit, Baptism is a bath that purifies, justifies, and sanctifies."[5] According to the Catechism of the Catholic Church, baptism purifies and justifies. It applies Christ in actuality to the person, bringing them into a state of justification. This view (stated clearly in the modern Catholic Catechism) is what the Reformers and Perkins sought to rebuke.

That is why Perkins maintained the view Calvin promoted as a proper view of baptism, not as a salvific act but as a sign of the salvific act of God. He writes concerning what baptism did as far as a sacrament:

> "The element of the water whereby the uncleanness of the body is purified by a most convenient proportion shadows out the blood of Christ and by the figure synecdoche, taking the part for the whole Christ ... The action of the minister

---

4. Perkins, William. *Combat between Christ and the Devil: Matthew 4:1-11.* Vol. 1 of The Works of William Perkins. Edited by J. Stephen Yuille. General Editors Joel R. Beeke and Derek W.H. Thomas. Grand Rapids, Michigan. Reformation Heritage Books. 2014, 88.

5. Catholic Catechism. Catechism of the Catholic Church—IntraText (vatican.va). Baptism and the Economy of Salvation, 1227.

> is his washing of the party baptized with the element of water. This seals and confirms a double action of God. (1) The engrafting or incorporating of the party baptized into Christ. (2) our spiritual regeneration."[6]

In Perkins' well-known work, *The Golden Chain*, he addresses this issue as well, clearly defining the Reformed view of baptism in contrast to Roman Catholic dogma. According to Perkins in *The Golden Chain*:

> "The action of the party to be baptized is twofold. The first is to offer himself to be baptized before the minister, and in the presence of the congregation. This signifies that he does consecrate himself to the Lord, and that he utterly renounces the flesh, the world, and the devil... The second is to receive the external washing by water. This signifies that the party baptized does receive the internal washing which is by the blood of Christ, or at the least that is offered to him."[7]

Notice he uses the language "signifies," not the language of "justification," which Rome would have promoted. Therefore, we can conclude, according to Perkins, baptism signified the reality of regeneration for the believer in Christ and conveyed such promises to the adherent, all to the glory of God.

Mode of baptism

How was baptism to be done? Was it by sprinkling? Immersion? How did Perkins address the mode of baptism? Was it to be *re*-performed in certain scenarios? Was he concerned about it? Perkins, in his time, did not have the great divergence of views that we may face today. However, he does write on this issue. Perkins writes on

---

6. Perkins, William. *Golden Chain. Vol. 6 of The Works of William Perkins.* Edited by Joel R. Beeke and Greg A. Salazar. General Editors Joel R. Beeke and Derek W.H. Thomas. Grand Rapids, Michigan. Reformation Heritage Books. 2018, 163.

7. Ibid., 164.

the reality of immersion and why it was no longer practiced for those of ripe profession (adult professors):

> "The ancient custom of baptizing was to dip and, as it were, to dive all the body of the baptized in the water, as may appear in Paul (Romans 6) and the councils of Laodicea and Neocaesarea. But now especially in cold countries, the church uses only to sprinkle the baptized by reason of children's weakness; for very few of ripe years are nowadays baptized. We need not much to marvel at this alteration, seeing charity and necessity may dispense with ceremonies and mitigate in equity the sharpness of them." [8]

He acknowledged the ancient custom was to dip or dive the body into the water according to Paul in Romans 6 and the councils of Laodicea and Neocaesarea. However, he conveys that sprinkling due to various needs in different contexts was a mode adapted. Perkins appears to believe that the mode was not as commanded. The focus was to be the action itself and its signification. He also was quick to refute any idea of rebaptism.

Perkins writes:

> "Rebaptizing is at no hand to be admitted; for as in natural generation man is once only born, so it is in spiritual regeneration. Therefore, they that are baptized of a minister which is a heretic not yet degraded from that calling (if the external form of administration be observed) must not be baptized again of the church of God, especially if after baptism they have been made partakers of the Lord's Supper." [9]

Perkins here is arguing that as regeneration happens once and baptism is a conveyance of that promise; therefore, it should not be undertaken more than once. He even believes if a heretic was conducting the baptism, the child or person need not be baptized again, especially if they had already partaken of the Lord's Supper. Perkins saw the validity of baptism not in the qualifications of the one delivering it (an early church discussion) but in the Word of

8. Ibid., 163.
9. Ibid., 164.

God that conveyed its meaning. Perkins' view of baptism carried forward Calvin's ideology and conveyed what many Puritans later held, as seen in the Westminster Confession of Faith. The Westminster Confession of 1647 with crystal clarity presents Perkins' view in concise and clear statements:

> "1. Baptism is a sacrament of the New Testament, ordained by Jesus Christ, not only for the solemn admission of the party baptized into the visible Church, but also to be unto him a sign and seal of the covenant of grace, of his ingrafting into Christ, of regeneration, of remission of sins, and of his giving up unto God, through Jesus Christ, to walk in newness of life: which sacrament is, by Christ's own appointment, to be continued in his Church until the end of the world. 2. The outward element to be used in this sacrament is water, wherewith the party is to be baptized in the name of the Father, and of the Son, and of the Holy Ghost, by a minister of the gospel lawfully called thereunto. 3. Dipping of the person into the water is not necessary; but baptism is rightly administered by pouring or sprinkling water upon the person. 4. Not only those that do actually profess faith in and obedience unto Christ, but also the infants of one or both believing parents are to be baptized. 5. Although it be a great sin to contemn or neglect this ordinance, yet grace and salvation are not so inseparably annexed unto it, as that no person can be regenerated or saved without it, or that all that are baptized are undoubtedly regenerated. 6. The efficacy of baptism is not tied to that moment of time wherein it is administered; yet, notwithstanding, by the right use of this ordinance the grace promised is not only offered, but really exhibited and conferred by the Holy Ghost, to such (whether of age or infants) as that grace belongeth unto, according to the counsel of God's own will, in his appointed time. 7. The sacrament of baptism is but once to be administered to any person." [10]

Notice the great similarities between the Westminster Confession and Perkins in all aspects of baptism, from what it is in section 1

---

10. Westminster Confession of Faith. Chapter 28: Of Baptism. Section 1-7.

to the clear teaching that baptism is not to be repeated in sections 6-7, where the validity or grace of baptism is not connected to its timing; rather, to its being tethered to the Word of God and God's grace conferred by the Holy Spirit's blessing of the sacrament to the faith of the recipient. The adult converts and children of Christians being the recipients put forth in section 4 of the Westminster statement on baptism matches what Calvin and Perkins themselves conveyed and expounded. Even the mode that Perkins was clear to address was conveyed in the concise language in Westminster in sections 2-3 above. The Westminster divines furthered Calvin's and Perkins' understanding in their Confession's codification of this doctrine. Perkins' influence can be traced to such a confession as many of his students (Thomas Goodwin, Samuel Ward, etc.) made up the members of such historical writing that became the Westminster Confession. Perkins' statements and teachings conveyed to such men as Goodwin and Ward made it to the pages of a document that is still in use today among faithful confessional churches across the Western world. While in the scope of this dissertation, there is much that could be said of Perkins passing the baton of faith to godly men who followed him and who took the baton further in the race than he did. Paul wrote in 2 Timothy 2:1-2, "You then, my child, be strengthened by the grace that is in Christ Jesus, and what you have heard from me in the presence of many witnesses entrust to faithful men, who will be able to teach others also."

Conclusion on Perkins' thought on baptism

Perkins held to what would later be defined in the Westminster Standards concerning baptism. It is clear that Perkins did not believe that baptism must be by immersion or subsequent to conversion. It was a sign and seal conveying the inward reality of regeneration. As outlined above, William Perkins writes:

> *"Baptism is a sacrament by which such as are within the covenant are washed with water in the name of the Father, the Son, and the Holy Ghost, that being thus engrafted into*

> *Christ they may have perpetual fellowship with Him . . . Within the covenant are all the seeds of Abraham or the seed of the faithful. These are either riper years or infants. Those of riper years are all such as adjoining themselves to the visible church do both testify their repentance of their sins and hold the foundations of religion taught in the same church . . . Infants within the covenant are such as have one at the least of their parents faithful."* [11]

Baptism, according to Perkins, was a sacrament. A sign and symbol to be done in the name of the Triune God and given to professors and their children. What made baptism valid, according to Perkins, was not its timing or the one who administered it. Rather it was the Word of God. Much is to be commended for his outlining of this sacrament according to Scripture.

---

11. Perkins, William. *Golden Chain. Vol. 6 of The Works of William Perkins.* Edited by Joel R. Beeke and Greg A. Salazar. General Editors Joel R. Beeke and Derek W.H. Thomas. Grand Rapids, Michigan. Reformation Heritage Books. 2018, 161-162.

Chapter Five

PERKINS' VIEW OF THE LORD'S SUPPER

IMAGINE BEING THERE WHEN Christ sat down with His disciples to partake of the last Passover meal He would share in as a Jewish man in the world. He looks at the elements and institutes that will be celebrated by the Church henceforth. The solemnity in the room must have been palpable. The Lord Jesus instituted in His Church on that night what has been labeled the Lord's Supper. During the Passover meal before His crucifixion, the Lord Jesus brought forth this institution as a fulfillment of what the Passover represented to Israel. We read in Matthew 26:26-29:

> "Now as they were eating, Jesus took bread, and after blessing it broke it and gave it to the disciples, and said, 'Take, eat; this is my body.' And he took a cup, and when he had given thanks he gave it to them, saying, 'Drink of it, all of you, for this is my blood of the covenant, which is poured out for many for the forgiveness of sins. I tell you I will not drink again of this fruit of the vine until that day when I drink it new with you in my Father's kingdom.'"

The Lord Jesus took the bread and the wine and defined this new sacrament in terms that the Church has cherished since its inception. The bread and wine convey the promises of God in the body of Christ and the blood of Christ given for the remission of the sins of the elect of God. The Lord's Supper is a conveyance of the faithfulness of God to His covenant people.

Roman Catholic and Protestant views of the Lord's Supper

The Lord Jesus instituted this sacrament not to grant salvation but to strengthen the faith of those who had salvation by grace through faith. Much of what Calvin, Perkins, and later Puritans would write was a recovery of the proper doctrine of this sacrament from the Romish error. Rome teaches (as it taught in Luther's, Calvin's, and Perkins' time) that the bread and wine become the actual body and blood of Christ. This is called the doctrine of *transubstantiation*. The Catholic Catechism puts it like this:

> "*1333 At the heart of the Eucharistic celebration are the bread and wine that, by the words of Christ and the invocation of the Holy Spirit, become Christ's Body and Blood.*" [1]

> "*1376 The Council of Trent summarizes the Catholic faith by declaring: "Because Christ our Redeemer said that it was truly his body that he was offering under the species of bread, it has always been the conviction of the Church of God, and this holy Council now declares again, that by the consecration of the bread and wine there takes place a change of the whole substance of the bread into the substance of the body of Christ our Lord and of the whole substance of the wine into the substance of his blood. This change the holy Catholic Church has fittingly and properly called transubstantiation.*" [2]

The Council of Trent reference in the Catechism was Rome's response in 1545-1563 to the Reformation. This council upheld the Romish teaching of transubstantiation, teaching that the

---

1. Catholic Catechism. Catechism of the Catholic Church—IntraText (vatican.va). Eucharist and the Economy of Salvation, 1333.

2. Catholic Catechism. Catechism of the Catholic Church—IntraText (vatican.va). The Sacramental Sacrifice Thanksgiving, Memorial, Presence, 1376.

PERKINS' VIEW OF THE LORD'S SUPPER

Reformers and the Puritans, after them, thoroughly opposed. In his work *Reformed Catholic*, Perkins makes abundantly clear his disdain for Rome's view of the Lord's Supper . He writes:

> *"They make the eucharist to be real, external, or bodily sacrifice offered unto God, holding and teaching that the minister is a priest properly, and that in this sacrament he offers Christ's body and blood to God the Father really and properly under the forms of bread and wine. We acknowledge no real, outward, or bodily sacrifice for the remission of sins, but only Christ's oblation on the cross once offered. Here is the main difference between us, touching this point. And it is of that weight and moment, that they stiffly maintaining their opinion (as they do) can be no church of God. For this point razes the foundation to the very bottom. And that it may the better appear that we avouch the truth, first, I will confirm our doctrine by Scripture, and second, confute the reasons which they bring for themselves."* [3]

Perkins had no qualms about the seriousness of Rome's error. Holding Rome's view of transubstantiation would mean not being a true church, and the very foundation of such a professing church was wrong. He strongly rejected Rome's view of the Lord's Supper, calling it a "fable." He writes:

> *"The doctrine of transubstantiation, which teaches that the bread is turned into the very body of Christ and the wine into His blood, is a very fable. The reasons why are these: (1) in the first institution of the Supper, which was before Christ's passion, the body of Christ was then eaten as already crucified. Now, how the body of Christ crucified should after a corporal manner be eaten He Himself being not as yet crucified, it is impossible to imagine. (2) The bread after the consecration is distributed into parts, but the whole body of Christ is received of every singular communicant. (3) The bread is the communion of Christ's body; therefore, not His very body. (4) By this means the*

---

3. Perkins, William. *Reformed Catholic. Vol. 7 of The Works of William Perkins.* Edited by Shawn D. Wright and Andrew S. Ballitch. General Editors Joel R. Beeke and Derek W.H. Thomas. Grand Rapids, Michigan. Reformation Heritage Books. 2019, 94.

body of Christ should not only be made of the substance of the Virgin Mary, but also of the baker's bread. (5) Let the bread and wine be kept for a time, and the bread will mold, and the wine turn to vinegar after the consecration—by which we may conclude that there did remain the substance of bread and wine. (6) This opinion quite overthrows the sacramental union—namely, the proportion which is between the sign and the thing signified." [4]

Perkins, in his work *The Problem of Forged Catholicism*, writes 22 points contradicting transubstantiation collected from the Church Fathers' writings, which he relied upon frequently in his writings. A summary of some of the reasons he gave is as follows:

"In ancient times it was the whole universal and orthodox consent of the church that that very bread which Christ broke (and not any other thing under the figure of bread) was His body. And this is the doctrine of Irenaeus, Justin Martyr, Tertullian, Cyprian, Theodoret, Chrysostom, Ambrose, and Augustine. And therefore, these never so much as dreamed of transubstantiation.... The words of Christ, 'my flesh is meat indeed' are by Clement; Tertullian, Origen, Chrysostom, and Augustine taken in the allegorical sense ... But the fathers speak not only figuratively of the sacrament, but even sometimes hyperbolically thereof, to beget it the greater reverence, and to pierce men's minds, and follow the phrase of Scripture, and lest the supper should seem a tragic fiction ... To consecrate is not to transubstantiate, but to dedicate a profane thing unto a holy use. And that the consecration of the bread is included in these five words, 'for this is my body,' and, of the wine in these, 'this is my blood,' or such like, no father did ever teach. Cyprian says that in his time they did consecrate with these words: 'Do this in remembrance of me; this is my flesh, this is my blood.' Basil and Chrysostom held that it was done by prayers we may read in their liturgies ... The body of Christ in the fathers' writings,

---

4. Perkins, William. *Golden Chain*. Vol. 6 of *The Works of William Perkins*. Edited by Joel R. Beeke and Greg A. Salazar. General Editors Joel R. Beeke and Derek W.H. Thomas. Grand Rapids, Michigan. Reformation Heritage Books. 2018, 168.

> is threefold: real, that is His body assumed; mystical, the church; sacramental, the bread and the supper . . . *The fathers say that we receive Christ in the bread, or under the form of bread, as the bread is a sign of Christ's flesh, and instrument of the soul's nourishment, not as the receptacle of His body* . . . *The sacrament is honored, received, and respected, as it is the expressive seal and sign of our mystical union with Christ, by whose body we are, after an admirable manner, quickened* . . . *The fathers give but one place at once unto Christ's body.* 'Our Lord is above,' says Augustine, tract 30. in Joh.
>
> Lastly, when transubstantiation was once established, the most learned stuck to the opinion of consubstantiation, either solely or chiefly, because the Church had so decreed. Scotus, in 4 dist. 11, q.3 art. 1, holds expressly that the doctrine of transubstantiation is not expressed in the Scriptures."[5]

Perkins' reference to the fathers was previously outlined in this dissertation, but its importance cannot be too strongly stated. He did not develop his understanding of the Christian faith apart from the historic creeds of the Church or the Patristic Fathers of the early Church. He stood on their shoulders. And on their shoulders, he clearly saw Rome's abuse of the Lord's Supper and their gross misinterpretation. Perkins made it clear that the Eucharist, in its ideology, was a re-sacrifice of Christ each time it was performed, which was blasphemous to John 19:30: "It is finished" of Christ Jesus on the cross.

Perkins was also unafraid to address his fellow Protestants as he developed his understanding of the Lord's Supper from the Holy Scripture and in light of the Patristic Fathers' teaching on the Scriptures. William Perkins strongly rejected Luther's view of the Lord's Supper: *consubstantiation*, as well. He writes:

---

5. Perkins, William. *The Problem of Forged Catholicism.* Vol. 7 of *The Works of William Perkins.* Edited by Shawn D. Wright and Andrew S. Ballitch. General Editors Joel R. Beeke and Derek W.H. Thomas. Grand Rapids, Michigan. Reformation Heritage Books. 2019, 308-333.

> "The like may be said of the Lutherans' consubstantiation, whereby they bear men in hand that there is a coexistence by which the body of Christ is either in or with or under the bread. Against this, these reasons may suffice: (1) the whole action of the Supper is done in remembrance of Christ. Now what need that, if the body of Christ were really present? (2) 'Whom the heavens must contain, until the time that all things must be restored' (Acts 3:21). (3) This is an essential property of every magnitude, and therefore of the body of Christ, to be in one place and circumcised or composed of one place. (4) If that Christ's body were eaten corporally, then should the wicked as well as the faithful be partakers of the flesh of Christ: but to eat His flesh is to believe in Him and to have eternal life. (5) It were very absurd to think that Christ, sitting among His disciples, did with His own hands take His own body and give it wholly to each of His disciples." [6]

He calls Luther's understanding of the Lord's Supper absurd in the sense that it was absurd to think that Christ, in instituting the Lord's Supper, did with His own hands take His own body and give it wholly to each of His disciples. His five reasons attack the heart of the illogical conclusions of the Lutheran movement with regard to the Lord's Supper. From the significance of the words Christ conveyed with regards to the Lord's Supper that it was to be done "In remembrance," Perkins posited that Christ could not bodily be present in the materials. He quotes Acts 3:21 to show that Christ is in His body in heaven until His return, which means His body is not in the Lord's Supper. It seemed Perkins, though grateful for Luther, was unafraid to address his differences with Luther's doctrine.

---

6. Perkins, William. *Golden Chain*. Vol. 6 of *The Works of William Perkins*, Edited by Joel R. Beeke and Greg A. Salazar. General Editors Joel R. Beeke and Derek W.H. Thomas. Grand Rapids, Michigan. Reformation Heritage Books. 2018, 168.

Conclusion of Perkins' thought on the Lord's Supper

Perkins believed the Lord's Supper was a sign and seal of the promises of God to the people of God redeemed in Christ by faith. He writes about the real presence of Christ in the sacrament of the Lord's Supper:

> *"In the sacrament, the body of Christ is received as it was crucified, and His blood as it was shed upon the cross. But now at this time, Christ's body crucified remains still as a body, but not as a body crucified, because the act of crucifying is ceased. Therefore, it is faith alone that makes Christ crucified to be present unto us in the sacrament."* [7]

He believed in the presence of Christ being the spiritual presence of Christ in the sacrament. Perkins writes:

> *"We hold and believe a presence of Christ's body and blood in the sacrament of the Lord's Supper, and that not feigned, but a true and real presence, which must be considered two ways: first, in respect of the signs; second, in respect of the communicants."* [8]

Notice his language here of "we" and "hold." This is confessional language that typified the view of the Puritans in his time—those who held to biblical convictions with the Gospel. He held to the presence of Christ's body and blood though not in the elements themselves. William Perkins' writes in his great work entitled *Golden Chain* on the Lord's Supper:

> *"The Lord's Supper is a sacrament wherewith in the signs of the bread and wine such as are engrafted into Christ are*

---

7. Perkins, William. *Reformed Catholic.* Vol. 7 of *The Works of William Perkins.* Edited by Shawn D. Wright and Andrew S. Ballitch. General Editors Joel R. Beeke and Derek W.H. Thomas. Grand Rapids, Michigan. Reformation Heritage Books. 2019, 88.

8. Perkins, William. *Reformed Catholic.* Vol. 7 of *The Works of William Perkins.* Edited by Shawn D. Wright and Andrew S. Ballitch. General Editors Joel R. Beeke and Derek W.H. Thomas. Grand Rapids, Michigan. Reformation Heritage Books. 2019, 85.

> in Him daily in a spiritual manner nourished to eternal life... The elements of bread and wine are signs and seals of the body and blood of Christ." [9]

In thinking through the Lord's Supper, he addressed who was to be its recipients, especially with his view of a pure Church (true, born-again Christians being the Church). William Perkins would go on to write on whom he believed, scripturally, was qualified to partake in the Lord's Supper from the congregation:

> "First a knowledge of God and man's fall and of the promised restoration into the covenant by Christ. Secondly, true faith in Christ for every man receives so much as he believes he receives. Thirdly, renewed faith and repentance for daily and new sins committed upon infirmity, because every new sin requires a new act both of repentance and faith." [10]

In essence, he believed that only those who had an authentic profession of faith and fruit-bearing witness to such a faith should partake of the Lord's Supper. Fruit such as ongoing repentance and faith; a faith that kept trusting in Christ; a faith that kept repenting of sin. This was the view that later Puritans held, as expressed in the Westminster Confession of Faith. The Westminster Confession of Faith, taking the same position that Perkins appears to posit, states:

> "I. Our Lord Jesus, in the night wherein He was betrayed, instituted the sacrament of His body and blood, called the Lord's Supper, to be observed in His Church, unto the end of the world, for the perpetual remembrance of the sacrifice of Himself in His death; the sealing all benefits thereof, unto true believers, their spiritual nourishment

---

9. Perkins, William. *Golden Chain. Vol. 6 of The Works of William Perkins.* Edited by Joel R. Beeke and Greg A. Salazar. General Editors Joel R. Beeke and Derek W.H. Thomas. Grand Rapids, Michigan. Reformation Heritage Books. 2018, 167.

10. Perkins, William. *Golden Chain. Vol. 6 of The Works of William Perkins.* Edited by Joel R. Beeke and Greg A. Salazar. General Editors Joel R. Beeke and Derek W.H. Thomas. Grand Rapids, Michigan. Reformation Heritage Books. 2018, 168-169.

and growth in Him, their further engagement in and to all duties which they owe unto Him; and, to be a bond and pledge of their communion with Him, and with each other, as members of His mystical body, (1Co 11:23-26; 1Co 10:16-17, 21; 1Co 12:13). II. In this sacrament, Christ is not offered up to His Father; nor any real sacrifice made at all, for remission of sins of the quick or dead, (Hbr 9:22, 25-26, 28); but only a commemoration of that one offering up of Himself, by Himself, upon the cross, once for all: and a spiritual oblation of all possible praise unto God, for the same, (1Co 11:24-26; Mat 26:26-27): so that the popish sacrifice of the mass (as they call it) is most abominably injurious to Christ's one, only sacrifice, the alone propitiation for all the sins of His elect, (Hbr 7:23-24, 27; Hbr 10:11-12, 14, 18)." [11]

Both Perkins and the divines who composed the Westminster Confession repudiated Romish teaching and defined the Lord's Supper for professors of the true Gospel and their spiritual nourishment. The Westminster divines, to their great credit, seemed to take great pains to convey, as quoted above, their exact stance, so that there would be no misunderstanding. Like Perkins, they wanted to be very clear—not ambiguous.

Once more, Perkins saw the sacraments and their proper modes and usage as vital to the health of the biblical church. He saw Rome's position as a gross error that demeaned Christ Jesus, and he would likely see some Protestants' flippancy in their usage today also as a gross evil. Perkins believed that the sacraments conveyed the promises of the Gospel and the glory of Christ. The only two sacraments are the Lord's Supper and Baptism. Baptism was the entrance into the visible church community, and the Lord's Supper, the table whereby the members of the church in fellowship with Christ and one another came for strength and grace from God to grow and endure in the faith.

To conclude, Perkins' view of the sacraments further developed Calvin's understanding and was later seen in the

---

11. Westminster Confession of Faith. Chapter 29: Of the Lord's Supper. Study Resources (blueletterbible.org) Section 1-2.

Westminster Confession of Faith. He stood against Rome in their sacramental system and even Luther's view of the Lord's Supper. The title "Father of the Puritans" seems to have some gravity to it, as Perkins, at the forefront of the great movement now referred to as the Puritan movement, exposited clearly defined doctrines that would be the hallmark of the blossoming movement that would inform not just England and certain European countries but the Colonies as well.

Chapter Six

PERKINS' VIEW OF PASTORAL MINISTRY

THE OFFICE OF THE pastor is a gift of the resurrected and ascended Jesus to the Church He loves. It is an office connected with "preaching the Word of God." An office that Perkins saw as sacred. Perkins writes, "All prophets and ministers are God's deputies and commissioners. It is, therefore, reason that they have authority from their Lord and Master."[1] This office, this authority, is our resurrected and ascended Lord's gift to His Church. In Ephesians 4:11-14 Paul writes:

> "And he gave the apostles, the prophets, the evangelists, the shepherds and teachers, to equip the saints for the work of ministry, for building up the body of Christ, until we all attain to the unity of the faith and of the knowledge of the Son of God, to mature manhood, to the measure of the stature of the fullness of Christ, so that we may no longer be children, tossed to and fro by the waves and carried about by every wind of doctrine, by human cunning, by craftiness in deceitful schemes."

---

1. Perkins, William. *Calling of the Ministry*. Vol. 10 of *The Works of William Perkins*. Edited by Joseph A. Pipa and J. Stephen Yuille. General Editors Joel R. Beeke and Derek W.H. Thomas. Grand Rapids, Michigan. Reformation Heritage Books. 2020, 278.

Paul outlines the three extraordinary gifts of God to the Church: apostles, prophets, and evangelists (apostolic representatives like Timothy and Titus). Extraordinary gifts have ceased since the Church's foundation has been laid for all time (Ephesians 2:19-21). One or two (depending on where a person lands in that discussion) of the offices that likewise are a gift alongside the other three extraordinary offices continue today: the office of pastor and the office of teacher. Now my objective here is not to debate whether the shepherd and teacher are the same or two different offices. Regardless, it can be universally agreed that pastor of a local church is included in the "shepherd and teacher" category and is a gift of God to the church. This office exists to see the elect come forth collected into the body of believers by faith, to see the church of God matured in the faith and established in truth so as to serve others in the name of the Lord Jesus. John Owen addressed this topic. In a sermon he stated:

> "*Gifts make no man a minister; but all the world cannot make a minister of Christ without gifts. If the Lord Jesus should cease to give out spiritual gifts unto men for the work of the ministry, he need do no more to take away the ministry itself; it must cease also: and it is the very way the ministry ceases in apostatizing churches—Christ no more giving out unto them of the gifts of his Spirit; and all their outward forms and order, which they can continue, are of signification in his sight.*" [2]

According to Owen, the Lord Jesus is the One who makes a man a minister. If Christ should take away His ministers from the church, according to Owen, the church would soon apostatize. This is a high view of the office of pastor. The pastor teaches the church, builds her up, sees her come into Christian maturity, and protects her from false teaching that would bring forth chaos and destruction in her Christian life and witness. Pastors and pastoral ministry are a gift of God to His people. God gifts

---

2. Owen, John. *Posthumous Sermons: The Ministry of Christ*. Vol. 9 of *The Works of John Owen*. (ed. William H. Goold. London: The Banner of Truth Trust. 1987), 432.

pastors for this task. This also means pastors and their faithfulness to the Word or lack thereof has a great impact on the life of the church. Pastors who have gone to be with the Lord are still impacting many today through their faithful work and writing. Their faithful teaching of the Word of God that is recorded for us in writings and sermons is still a gift of God to us, the church. Albert Martin, a reformed Baptist pastor whose ministry was primarily in the twentieth century, writes:

> "God has given to the church in past days and in our own day men whose ministries have been particularly owned as 'masters of the inner life,' as I like to call them. I am referring to those men to whom God has given unusual insights concerning the struggles of the soul, the windings of remaining sin, the wiles of the devil, and the things that will keep us fresh in our relationship to the Lord. Such men are God's gift to me, and I ought to prayerfully, wisely, and judiciously own and use them, not as masters of my faith, but as helpers to my faith. When I speak of things written by masters of the inner life, I am referring to John Owen's volumes on *The Glory of Christ* (vol.1), *Communion with God* (vol. 2), *Indwelling Sin, Temptation and Mortification of Sin* (vol. 6), and *Spiritual-Mindedness* (vol. 7); John Flavel's treatise on *Keeping the Heart*; Thomas Brooks's *Precious Remedies Against Satan's Devices* and *The Secret Key to Heaven*; John Bunyan's treatise on *Prayer*; The works of Sibbes; Baxter's *The Reformed Pastor*; Scudder on *The Christian's Daily Walk*; Octavius Winslow's works; *The Glory of the Redeemer* and *The Precious Things of God*." [3]

These works Martin references were mainly done by Shepherds and Teachers, and most of them were directly or indirectly influenced by Perkins' own thought and teaching on the Scriptures, as outlined earlier in this dissertation. Martin's life was impacted by these men who had long been with the Lord in glory. Perkins being at the forefront of a movement that produced "masters of the

---

3. Martin, Albert N. *Pastoral Theology*. Volume 1. Trinity Pulpit Press. Montville, New Jersey. 2018, 281.

inner life," as Martin describes, warrants examination. It is helpful for us to ask, "How did Perkins view the pastoral ministry?"

What did Perkins believe about pastoral ministry as a gift of the Lord Jesus to the church? Perkins, in *The Duties and Dignity of the Ministry* from the text of Job 33:23-24, outlines the description of a true minister of the Gospel in five ways:

> "1. By his titles, which are two: 'angel' 'interpreter.' 2. By his rarity: 'one of a thousand.' 3. By his office: 'to declare unto men his righteousness.' 4. By the blessing that God gives upon the labors of this true minister: 'then God will have mercy upon the sinner.' 5. By His commission and authority in the last words: God will say, 'Deliver him that he go not down into the pit, for I have received a reconciliation.'" [4]

Perkins applied the truths found in Job 33:23-24 to pastoral ministry and its purposes. He saw the phrases as a good descriptor of true pastors as gifts of God to the church. He describes the rarity of such a true gift by calling a pastor from the text "one of the thousand." This phrase was meant to be awe-striking. A true pastor is a rare person. Not many are this type of person, according to Perkins. Later in this book, he argues that because true pastors are a rare gift, the church should appreciate them, cherish their ministry, and see their ministry as a blessing to them from the Lord Jesus, who loves His Church. Perkins highly valued the office, though he himself never moved from the position of lecturer, likely due to circumstances in the Church of England at the time. He called the pastor an angel or interpreter; one who is a messenger of God Himself. An ambassador of the King of angel armies. His meaning is clear: the pastor is a messenger of Christ to Christ's church. He belongs to Christ and is sent to God's elect in the world. He does not exist for the world but for the people of God, whom God is calling out of the world. His duties are not to be an innovative visionary, a great leader, or a profoundly

---

4. Perkins, William. *Calling of the Ministry.* Vol. 10 of *The Works of William Perkins.* Edited by Joseph A. Pipa and J. Stephen Yuille. General Editors Joel R. Beeke and Derek W.H. Thomas. Grand Rapids, Michigan. Reformation Heritage Books. 2020, 204.

motivating speaker. As Perkins points out, the pastor is a steward of the message Christ gave, and it is those such labors that God ordained only to bless. The pastor's message declares righteousness and reconciliation. His life must correspond to his message. His commission is clear. His King's victory, sure.

An educated clergy

Reading Perkins' description of the office of pastor and its high calling, one can easily ask, "Who is capable of such a thing?" Perkins believed men entering ministry must be prepared for such a high calling. Part of Perkins' answer to such a query would have been that a pastor must be set apart and trained. Perkins believed in a thoroughly educated clergy. In his commentary on Galatians, he outlined in detail the importance of a properly taught clergy, which was a problem that he noted for those who proceeded generations after the apostles. He writes, "For teachers themselves must first learn, and then teach."[5] He noted that teachers of the Word must first have been taught the Word themselves. He emphasized that there were no shortcuts to proper ministry. Diligent preparation was required and vital to the faithfulness of a pastor. The language of feeling called and sent immediately to preach would have been abominable to Perkins and all the Puritans. Perkins writes:

> "If every true minister must be God's interpreter to the people, and the people's to God, then hence we learn that everyone, who either is or intends to be a minister, must have that tongue of the learned which is spoken of in Isaiah 50:4. Here the prophet says (first, in the name of Christ, as He is the great Prophet and Teacher of His church, and, second, in the name of himself and all true prophets while the world endures), 'The Lord God hath

---

5. Perkins, William. *Commentary on Galatians. Vol. 2 of The Works of William Perkins*. Edited by Paul M. Smalley. General Editors Joel R. Beeke and Derek W.H. Thomas. Grand Rapids, Michigan. Reformation Heritage Books. 2015, 45.

*given me a tongue of the learned, that I should know to speak a word in season to him that is weary."*⁶

For Perkins, an uneducated clergy would be a great harm to the Church, as she would be unable to discern the deceitful teachings and false ideologies of man (Ephesians 4:14). He understood the importance of pastors knowing their Bibles, their faith, their historical theology, and the heresies that had threatened the Church for ages. The pastor was no less than an ambassador of Christ to the people of Christ. He advocated for a model of ministry that trained pastors in a rigorous academic setting combined with accountability that promoted true piety and holiness of heart and life among the clergymen. He would have been disheartened by much of modern pastors' lack of training in the faith and Church history as well as the antinomianism of our time.

Perkins' thought on the minister as an ambassador of God was embraced and perpetuated in later generations, even up to the time of Lloyd-Jones in the twentieth century. Martyn Lloyd-Jones, in his book *Preaching and Preachers*, states this about true pastoral preaching rooted in the truth of 2 Timothy 2:15:

> "Any true definition of preaching must say that man is there to deliver the message of God, a message from God to those people. If you prefer the language of Paul, he is 'an ambassador for Christ'. That is what he is. He has been sent, he is a commissioned person, and he is standing there as the mouthpieces of God and of Christ to address these people... Preaching, in other words, is a transaction between the preacher and the listener. It does something for the soul of man, for the whole of the person, the entire man; it deals with him in a vital and radical manner." [7]

---

6. Perkins, William. *Calling of the Ministry.* Vol. 10 of *The Works of William Perkins.* Edited by Joseph A. Pipa and J. Stephen Yuille. General Editors Joel R. Beeke and Derek W.H. Thomas. Grand Rapids, Michigan. Reformation Heritage Books. 2020, 208.

7. Lloyd-Jones, Martyn. *Preaching and Preachers.* (London: Hodder and Stoughton. 1971), 53.

Lloyd Jones here captures what Perkins describes in his writings as the pastor being the "angel," the "messenger" of Christ to His people. He is not a messenger as one who receives direct revelation. He is expounding the once-and-for-all delivered message to Christ's people and applying it to their consciences. The pastor's preaching is to call forth from the people of God obedience to Christ in their wills and a delighting of Christ from their affections.

Pastors must know the flock they are charged to care for

Perkins believed pastors had to know their people's life situations and needs. He must minister to those people where they are in their life, family, work, and daily trials. A pastor, according to Perkins, must know his people. He writes:

> "First, to teach that it is the minister's duty to confess, not only his own sins, but the sins of his people, and to complain of them to God. For as he is the people's interpreter to God, he must not think it enough to put up their petitions, to unfold their wants, and to crave relief for them at God's hand, but he must further take knowledge of the sins of his people, and make both public and private confession of them to God... And if the minister ought to know his people's sins, then it follows, first, that it is best for a minister to be present with his people, so that he may better know them and their state." [8]

Perkins would have rejected any model of ministry where the pastor was more of a CEO or manager of a force of volunteers to accomplish given tasks and goals. He would not have understood this idea of a pastor not knowing his people's names and life scenarios and would have resisted large settings as entertainment

---

8. Perkins, William. *Calling of the Ministry. Vol. 10 of The Works of William Perkins.* Edited by Joseph A. Pipa and J. Stephen Yuille. General Editors Joel R. Beeke and Derek W.H. Thomas. Grand Rapids, Michigan. Reformation Heritage Books. 2020, 244-245.

centers at the worst and preaching points at the best. He, like most Puritans, believed that pastors must know their people. John Owen, influenced by Perkins' thought here, would later write in his book *True Nature of a Gospel Church*:

> "A prudent and diligent consideration of the state of the flock over which any man is set, as unto their strength or weaknesses, their growth or defect in knowledge (the measure of their attainments requiring either milk or strong meat), their temptations and duties, their spiritual decays or thrivings; and that not only in general, but, as near as may be, with respect unto all the individual members of the church. Without a due regard unto these things, men preach at random, uncertainly fighting, like those that beat the air. Preaching sermons not designed for the advantage of them to whom they are preached; insisting on general doctrines not levelled to the condition of the auditory; speaking what men can, without consideration of what they ought,—are things that will make men weary of preaching, when their minds are not influenced with outward advantages, as much as make others weary in hearing them." [9]

Owen understood that the undershepherding oversight of the flock had significant ramifications for the flock's well-being and growth, which is why the pastor must know his people. Owen lived what he wrote, as he spent his later years caring for a smaller flock. After his university career, Owen focused his time and passion on pastoring Leadenhall Chapel in London, which he pastored faithfully until he died in 1683, a few years before the Act of Toleration of 1689 went into effect. We see Owen's heart for his own people in a letter that he wrote to them in 1680. He addressed them as "Beloved in the Lord" and then penned the following second part to his opening:

> "But although I am absent from you in body, I am in mind, affection and spirit present with you, and in your

---

9. Owen, John. *True Nature of a Gospel Church*. Vol. 16. of *The Works of John Owen*. (ed. William H. Goold. London: The Banner of Truth Trust. 1981), 76-77.

assemblies; for I hope you will be found my crown and rejoicing in the day of the Lord: and my prayer for you night and day is, that you may stand fast in the whole will of God, and maintain the beginning of your confidence without wavering, firm unto the end. I know it is needless for me at this distance to write to you about what concerns you in point of duty at this season, that work being well supplied by my brother in the ministry; yet give me leave, out of my abundant affections towards you, to bring some few things to your remembrance as my weakness will permit."[10]

He ended the letter and signed it in the following way: "Your unworthy pastor and your servant for Jesus' sake. J. Owen."[11] John Owen, on this issue of pastors knowing their flocks assigned by the Lord Jesus, the Chief Shepherd to whom they belong, was clear in practice and admonition. He writes:

"Let the ministers engage themselves in a special manner to watch over his flock, everyone according to his abilities, both in teaching, exhorting, and ruling, so often as occasion shall be administered, for things that contain ecclesiastical rule and church order; acting jointly and as in a classical combination, and putting forth all authority that such cases are intrusted with." [12]

Owen saw the pastors as those who must watch over a particular flock of Christ under Christ's rule. Perkins had stressed such an idea years before. This was revolutionary in contrast to the Roman view of clergy, who were disconnected from the people. Perkins understood that a pastor must know his flock and take the once-and-for-all delivered canon of Scripture to their consciences and present it to the eyes of their hearts. He believed that a pastors' highest desire for the local flock of God should be to see the

10. Barrett, Matthew. Michael A. G. Haykin. *Owen on the Christian Life: Living for the Glory of God in Christ*. Wheaton, IL: Crossway. 2015, 267.

11. Ibid., 267.

12. Owen, John. *A Country Essay: For the Practice of Church Government*. Vol. 8. of *The Works of John Owen*. (ed. William H. Goold. London: The Banner of Truth Trust. 1982), 51.

members of that local church be a people who strive diligently for godliness. He saw it worth the sacrifice. He writes:

> "And here such ministers as have poor livings but good people, let them not faint nor be discouraged. They have more cause to bless God than to be grieved, for doubtless they are far better than those who have great livings and an evil people." [13]

According to Perkins, a pastor must consider it a blessing to be among "good" people and not be discouraged, for that was far better than being among an ungodly group and well-paid. A flock, though small, that was godly was a crown on the head of a faithful pastor, according to Perkins. Perkins' statements here echo the focus of the Apostle Paul in 2 Corinthians 12:14-15 when he writes:

> "Here for the third time I am ready to come to you. And I will not be a burden, for I seek not what is yours but you. For children are not obligated to save up for their parents, but parents for their children. I will most gladly spend and be spent for your souls. If I love you more, am I to be loved less?"

A faithful pastor was to desire to see the flock of the Lord Jesus flourish in godliness and holiness. According to Perkins, the pastor himself was to model such behavior. Perkins writes: "Furthermore, inasmuch as ministers are interpreters, they must labor for sanctity and holiness of life."[14] It was not okay for a pastor to preach something and then habitually live in contradiction. Such a life would harm the pastor's ministry and undermine the message's validity. Holiness of life was non-negotiable for Perkins. He would have urged pastors to kill heart lusts. Lewis Allen, in his helpful book for pastors written in the time of this dissertation entitled *The Preacher's Catechism*, stated, concerning the heart-lusts of the pastor which drives the pastors' fears:

---

13. Perkins, William. *Calling of the Ministry*. Vol. 10 of *The Works of William Perkins*. Edited by Joseph A. Pipa and J. Stephen Yuille. General Editors Joel R. Beeke and Derek W.H. Thomas. Grand Rapids, Michigan. Reformation Heritage Books. 2020, 248.

14. Ibid, 209.

> "But there is a clean-hands and pure-bodies adultery that no one sees and is seldom confessed or even recognized. And that is the preacher's heart-lust for Something Else. Something Else? It's that congregation, that situation, that success, that appreciation (and maybe that wage) which we don't currently have. Whether Something Else is a real person or place, or just an imagined one, a preacher's temptation is to take his heart's love from what God has given him and to set it on what he believes he is entitled to. We never meant to do it. But it's happened to us, and we feel helpless. Maybe we're willing captives of our feelings. We nurture them, and we reason that, because we have them, they must be right—and that we really must be that good at preaching to know we're entitled to Something Else. Adultery isn't the main sin, though: doubting God's goodness is." [15]

Allen captures much of what tempts pastors today. Ambition, success, etc. Allen trumpets here what Perkins did hundreds of years earlier. For Perkins, the pastor's ambition should be holiness and faithfulness to Christ. His exhortation, by inference, to us today would be a call for pastors to be holy as the Lord is holy. To pursue holiness as an example. To kill heart-lusts. To desire Christ above all. According to his writings, this is what was behind Perkins' life and ministry.

Pastors protect the flock

Perkins saw the minister not as one who seeks great things for himself but seeks to honor the Lord Jesus as the "angel" or "ambassador" of Christ. The pastor is to declare Christ Jesus and maintain the truth against all gainsayers and false teachers. He writes in his discourse on the office of the minister:

> "First, a true minister may and must declare unto a sinful man where righteousness is to be found, namely, in 'Jesus Christ the righteous.' Second, how that righteousness may

---

15. Allen, Lewis. *The Preacher's Catechism.* Wheaton, Illinois: Crossway. 2018, 146.

> *be obtained, namely, by doing two duties: (1) by denying and disclaiming his own righteousness, and that is done by repentance; (2) by claiming and cleaving to Christ's righteousness, and that is done by faith. Third, a true minister may and must 'declare this righteousness to him.' First publish and proclaim that it is ready to be bestowed on every sinner who will thus apprehend it, and that is able to justify and save him . . . Besides declaration and testification, he is to maintain this truth and this righteousness against all gainsayers, against the power of darkness and all the gates of hell, that this is true and perfect righteousness to him who apprehends it, as afore is laid down. And this is so infallible to every soul who repents and believes."* [16]

Perkins saw it as part of the pastor's duty to protect the flock against what he calls "gain sayers": to protect the flock and define the truth so that false teachings may be refuted and disregarded for the good of the church. The pastor was to be a man who conveyed how righteousness was to be obtained through repentance and cleaving to Christ. He was a man who was about calling people unto Christ. Ministers were given a holy task as a gift to the church; therefore, pastors are to handle this ministry with the greatest of care. Perkins writes:

> *"Ministers themselves here must learn, when they take the word of reconciliation into their hands and mouths, to call to mind whose it is, even the Lord's, and that He works with them and has the greatest hand in the work, and that therefore they must use it in holy manner with much fear and reverence. It is not their own. They may not use it as they list."* [17]

---

16. Perkins, William. *Calling of the Ministry.* Vol. 10 of *The Works of William Perkins.* Edited by Joseph A. Pipa and J. Stephen Yuille. General Editors Joel R. Beeke and Derek W.H. Thomas. Grand Rapids, Michigan. Reformation Heritage Books. 2020, 218.

17. Perkins, William. *Calling of the Ministry.* Vol. 10 of *The Works of William Perkins.* Edited by Joseph A. Pipa and J. Stephen Yuille. General Editors Joel R. Beeke and Derek W.H. Thomas. Grand Rapids, Michigan. Reformation Heritage Books. 2020, 223.

PERKINS' VIEW OF PASTORAL MINISTRY

What was Perkins' view of pastoral ministry? Well, whether it was from house to house or from gathering to gathering, the pastor was to care for the people of God that he knew well, taking the Word of truth to them as the interpreter and angel (according to his writings as outlined above) to see them embrace Christ by faith, and grow in godliness and faithfulness, all to the glory of God. When we look around at all the books today on Christian leadership and how to motivate and lead people and teams, we can certainly appreciate God's common grace to us, but could it be that we have lost what it means to be a pastor who gives his life in service for the flock of Christ. To know that flock. To love that flock. To care for that flock. To counsel that flock. To preach to that flock. To pray for that flock. To live out the faith before that flock. To die, if Christ ordains, in service to that flock. Is that not the same pattern we see in the Chief Shepherd? He loves His flock. He cares for His flock. He comforts and counsels His flock by His Word and Spirit. He proclaims the truth to His flock through His Word. He still prays for the flock in intercession. He lived out a perfect example for the flock to the glory of God. He died for His flock. Undershepherds are supposed to model in a limited way the Chief Shepherd. Perhaps a return to the old ways would see a return to the deep joy of Christ that many of the pastors of the past both enjoyed and proclaimed.

Conclusion

William Perkins thoughts on pastoral ministry convey a strong view of the clergy knowing the Word and knowing the people God has entrusted to their care. Instead of an uneducated clergy, Perkins believed that the Bible commended an educated clergy. Perkins rightly understands the implication of Paul's words to Timothy in 2 Timothy 2:1-2:

> *"You then, my child, be strengthened by the grace that is in Christ Jesus, and what you have heard from me in the presence of many witnesses entrust to faithful men, who will be able to teach others also."*

Pastors are to be trained in the natural implication of what Paul says to Timothy in 2 Timothy 2. The faith must be taught and passed down to faithful men. Perkins' view fits the scriptural imperative. A needed reminder today.

A lot of Perkins' thought revolves around the clergy knowing well the flock's state. The clergyman must know the people. He must be educated in the Word and informed concerning the life of his people. To neglect either is to neglect his duty. We read the heart of 1 Peter 5:1-4 in Perkins' writings. Let us compare Perkins and Peter for a moment. Peter writes:

> *"So I exhort the elders among you, as a fellow elder and a witness of the sufferings of Christ, as well as a partaker in the glory that is going to be revealed: shepherd the flock of God that is among you, exercising oversight, not under compulsion, but willingly, as God would have you; not for shameful gain, but eagerly; not domineering over those in your charge, but being examples to the flock. And when the chief Shepherd appears, you will receive the unfading crown of glory."*

Perkins writes:

> *"First, to teach that it is the minister's duty to confess, not only his own sins, but the sins of his people, and to complain of them to God. For as he is the people's interpreter to God, he must not think it enough to put up their petitions, to unfold their wants, and to crave relief for them at God's hand, but he must further take knowledge of the sins of his people, and make both public and private confession of them to God . . . And if the minister ought to know his people's sins, then it follows, first, that it is best for a minister to be present with his people, so that he may better know them and their state."* [18]

Perkins clearly upholds Peter's exhortation to "shepherd the flock" among the elders in this text. With the rise of social media,

---

18. Perkins, William. *Calling of the Ministry. Vol. 10 of The Works of William Perkins.* Edited by Joseph A. Pipa and J. Stephen Yuille. General Editors Joel R. Beeke and Derek W.H. Thomas. Grand Rapids, Michigan. Reformation Heritage Books. 2020, 244-245.

which provides platforms to get messages and content out into the world rapidly, a reminder from men like Perkins may be in order. This is a reminder that "likes" on a sermon recorded via Facebook, views on a blog post, the number of sermon downloads from a website, as well as Twitter (now called "X") and Instagram followers, are not what ministers are commissioned to be about. According to Perkins, we are commissioned to care for a particular flock of Christ Jesus, not striving for our ministry to be about "helping" the flock in other men's care. If God should grant wider influence in our ministry as he did men like Whitefield, then may it be said that God did it, not a man's marketing prowess. However, Perkins would admonish us to focus on the flock of Christ Jesus among us. To pour into them the apostolic deposit. Peter's admonition in 1 Peter 5:1-4 supports Perkins' focus in ministry. May God grant reformation of the ministry to such a standard where pastors are focused on the flocks charged to them. To see them know Christ and be built up in Christ.

Perkins' pastoral ministry ideology revolves around these twin towers, educated in the Word and knowing the people of God, and he rightly emphasizes these twin truths. May God open the eyes of His undershepherds to such a high calling today.

— Chapter Seven —

PERKINS' VIEW OF PASTORAL PREACHING

BEFORE WE LOOK AT Perkins' view of pastoral preaching, we need to set some groundwork on pastoral preaching and its imperative. To preach the Gospel is the highest calling a man undergoes in this life. My mentor used to say, "If I were to become the president of the United States, it would be but a step down from the pastorate." A herald of the Word of God has a privileged and joyful calling, though a position filled with much opposition. A pastor is a herald whom God calls to preach to a particular people. In his book True Nature of a Gospel Church, Owen writes on the importance of faithful preaching in the local church, being the truth of God applied to the people of God. He writes as we have seen:

> "A prudent and diligent consideration of the state of the flock over which any man is set, as unto their strength or weaknesses, their growth or defect in knowledge (the measure of their attainments requiring either milk or strong meat), their temptations and duties, their spiritual decays or thrivings; and that not only in general, but, as near as may be, with respect unto all the individual members of the church. Without a due regard unto these things, men preach at random, uncertainly fighting, like

> *those that beat the air. Preaching sermons not designed for the advantage of them to whom they are preached; insisting on general doctrines not levelled to the condition of the auditory; speaking what men can, without consideration of what they ought,—are things that will make men weary of preaching, when their minds are not influenced with outward advantages, as much as make others weary in hearing them."* [1]

Owen understood that preaching was how God's truth was brought to bear on the souls of men and women. To proclaim the message of God is the primary task of preaching. Paul writes in Romans 10:13-17:

> *"For 'everyone who calls on the name of the Lord will be saved.' How then will they call on him in whom they have not believed? And how are they to believe in him of whom they have never heard? And how are they to hear without someone preaching? And how are they to preach unless they are sent? As it is written, 'How beautiful are the feet of those who preach the good news!' But they have not all obeyed the gospel. For Isaiah says, 'Lord, who has believed what he has heard from us?' So faith comes from hearing, and hearing through the word of Christ."*

Paul is quick to point out that faith comes by hearing and hearing through the Word of Christ (verse 17). Those who preach the Word of Christ (verse 15) are those sent by Christ, and how beautiful indeed are their feet that come to bring the Word of God. For all who call on the name of the Lord will be saved (verse 13), and they call on the name of the Lord because they hear the Gospel proclaimed and God's grace gives them spiritual life, resulting in faith (verse 17, Ephesians 2:1-10, Titus 3:4-5). What is amazing about this whole concept is that God has chosen preaching to be the primary means of the spiritual benefit of His elect, bringing them into the fold and strengthening them as

---

1. Owen, John. *True Nature of a Gospel Church*. Vol. 16. of *The Works of John Owen*. (ed. William H. Goold, London: The Banner of Truth Trust. 1981), 76-77.

they sojourn to the celestial city of God. Paul acknowledges the wonder of this in 1 Corinthians 1:21-25:

> *"For since, in the wisdom of God, the world did not know God through wisdom, it pleased God through the folly of what we preach to save those who believe. For Jews demand signs and Greeks seek wisdom, but we preach Christ crucified, a stumbling block to Jews and folly to Gentiles, but to those who are called, both Jews and Greeks, Christ the power of God and the wisdom of God. For the foolishness of God is wiser than men, and the weakness of God is stronger than men."*

Paul points out that God was pleased to choose what human eyes called "folly" to save those who believe. Many Jews, in their natural state, saw Christ crucified as a stumbling block. The Gentiles saw it as foolish. However, it was Christ crucified and this Gospel preaching that was the wisdom and means of God unto the salvation of God's elect. This high view of preaching produced one of the strongest exhortations given in all of the New Testament. Paul writes in 2 Timothy 4:1-2:

> *"I charge you in the presence of God and of Christ Jesus, who is to judge the living and the dead, and by his appearing and his kingdom: preach the word; be ready in season and out of season; reprove, rebuke, and exhort, with complete patience and teaching."*

Paul did not just tell Timothy to "preach the Word," but he undergirded it with a solemn oath "I charge you in the presence of God and of Christ Jesus." This conveys that preaching was vital and of the greatest importance. It is the means God primarily uses to draw and shape His sheep for Christ's glory and praise. The Westminster Confession of Faith emphasizes the important elements of the Lord's Day gathering for the church. Reading Scripture and its proclamation was the first emphasized. The Confession states:

> *"The reading of the Scriptures with godly fear; the sound preaching, and conscionable hearing of the Word, in obedience unto God with understanding, faith, and reverence;*

> *singing of psalms with grace in the heart; as, also, the due administration and worthy receiving of the sacraments instituted by Christ; are all parts of the ordinary religious worship of God: besides religious oaths, and vows, solemn fastings, and thanksgivings upon special occasions; which are, in their several times and seasons, to be used in an holy and religious manner."* [2]

The Westminster divines saw the reading and proclamation of the Word of God as the central part of the gathering of God's people and a non-negotiable necessity for the local church's health. Thomas Goodwin writes concerning preaching and its weightiness, "That the preaching of the gospel is an ordinance of Jesus Christ."[3] Goodwin rightly saw preaching as an ordinance of the Lord Jesus, an ordinance being an authoritative decree and issuance for the church to adhere to and receive. This was why the pulpit replaced the table in the center of most buildings where churches gathered during the Reformation into the Puritan era.

Perkins' understanding of the imperative of preaching

William Perkins had much to say concerning preaching, similar to what the Westminster Confession of Faith would have later said. Perkins' high view of preaching can be seen in his exposition of the Christian Religion as he writes:

> *"What is the use of the word of God preached? First, it breeds and then it increases faith in them which are chosen to salvation (Romans 1:17; 2 Corinthians 2:16; Hebrews 4:2) But unto them that perish it is by reason of their corruption an occasion of their further damnation."* [4]

---

2. Westminster Confession of Faith. Chapter 21: Of Religious Worship and the Sabbath Day. Section 5.

3. Goodwin, Thomas. The Government of the Churches of Christ. The Works of Thomas Goodwin. Volume 11. Soli Deo Gloria. Grand Rapids, Michigan. 2021, 359.

4. Perkins, William. *The Foundation of Christian Religion. Vol. 5 of The*

He stressed the imperative of preaching and wrote an entire book (likely his most famous work today outside of the *Golden Chain*) on proper preaching in all its aspects entitled *The Art of Prophesying*. In this book, Perkins conveyed the weightiness of preaching the Word of God as a minister of the Gospel. He writes:

> "That common place of divinity, which concerns the framing of sermons, is both weighty and difficult, if there is any other throughout all that sacred science. For the matter, which it is to explicate and treat on, is prophecy, an excellent gift indeed, whether we consider it in respect of dignity or use... Answerable to this dignity there is also a twofold use: (1) in that it serves to collect the church and to accomplish the number of the elect; (2) in that it drives away the wolves from the folds of the Lord."[5]

Notice he describes preaching as weighty and challenging. He would have seen preaching here both as a blessing and a burden. He referred to framing sermons as "sacred science," which means he believed there was a proper and an improper methodology. Exegetical methodology was a topic he went into depth on in *The Art of Prophesying* as he outlined how to interpret various literary genres of Scripture from Old Testament narrative to New Testament epistle. He gave examples of how to handle metaphorical language and appropriately apply it. Sermon preparation had a clear methodological framework for Perkins. The desired outcome was clear: exposition of the Scripture that rightly conveyed what God had said and was precisely applied to the conscience and lives of the listeners in the congregation.

He saw proper preaching as that which "serves to collect the church" and simultaneously "drives away the wolves from the folds of the Lord." Biblical preaching for Perkins was to see the

---

Works of William Perkins. Edited by Ryan Hurd. General Editors Joel R. Beeke and Derek W.H. Thomas. Grand Rapids, Michigan. Reformation Heritage Books. 2017, 505.

5. Perkins, William. *The Art of Prophesying*. Vol. 10 of *The Works of William Perkins*. Edited by Joseph A. Pipa and J. Stephen Yuille. General Editors Joel R. Beeke and Derek W.H. Thomas. Grand Rapids, Michigan. Reformation Heritage Books. 2020, 285.

elect saved and to drive away the goats from the Chief Shepherd's house, to guard the sheep, to protect them. There is much that can be learned here from Perkins' understanding that is necessary for our time. A lot of sermons and preaching are judged by how large the crowds attending are. Perkins would have seen a sermon's fruitfulness not in crowds gathered but in spiritual life produced in the elect. He also would have seen the fruit of a faithful sermon as that which drives out the wolf or goat from the flock. Preaching was not just a New Testament ideal, either, according to Perkins, but part of God's work in the world throughout redemptive history and His means of drawing His people to Himself. Perkins writes in his work on the Sermon on the Mount:

> "We must remember that preaching of the Word, though it be by sinful man, is God's holy ordinance, prescribed and enjoined as solemnly as any moral precept is either against murder or adultery; for from the beginning till the Jews came to Mount Sinai God Himself preached to His church." [6]

It is clear from such a statement that Perkins viewed preaching, even by sinful men, as God's holy ordinance and just as imperative as any moral precept such as "do not commit murder" from the Law of God. At this point, we need to define preaching and Perkins' view.

What exactly is preaching?

Paul writes in 2 Timothy 4:2, "Preach the word; be ready in season and out of season; reprove, rebuke, and exhort, with complete patience and teaching." What does Paul mean by "preach the Word"? Is preaching merely conveying doctrinal truth? Is preaching a transfer of information? Is it a motivational charge of sorts from Bible principles? Martyn Lloyd-Jones, in his book *Preaching and*

---

6. Perkins, William. *Sermon on the Mount: Matthew 5-7. Vol. 1 of The Works of William Perkins*. Edited by J. Stephen Yuille. General Editors Joel R. Beeke and Derek W.H. Thomas. Grand Rapids, Michigan. Reformation Heritage Books. 2014, 313.

Preachers, states this about true pastoral preaching rooted in the truth of 2 Timothy 2:15:

> "Any true definition of preaching must say that man is there to deliver the message of God, a message from God to those people. If you prefer the language of Paul, he is 'an ambassador for Christ'. That is what he is. He has been sent, he is a commissioned person, and he is standing there as the mouthpiece of God and of Christ to address these people . . . Preaching, in other words, is a transaction between the preacher and the listener. It does something for the soul of man, for the whole of the person, the entire man; it deals with him in a vital and radical manner." [7]

Preaching, according to Lloyd-Jones, was the delivering of a message from God to His people. It is a transaction between the preacher and the listener. It is the delivery of God's truth to the mind in order to, by the power of the Holy Spirit, raise the affections and drive the will to the Lord Jesus in faith that produces obedience. Spurgeon lamented the state of many pastors in his time when he spoke to the pastors' college (his last address delivered before his death):

> "Nowadays, we have a class of people around us who preach Christ, and even preach the gospel, but then preach a great deal else which is not true, and thus they destroy the good of all that they deliver, and lure men to error. They would be styled 'evangelical' and yet be part of the school which is really anti-evangelical. Watch out for these people. I have heard that a fox, when hunted closely by dogs, will pretend to be one of them, and run with the pack. That is what certain people are aiming for right now: the foxes would seem to be dogs. But in the case of the fox, his strong scent betrays him, and the dogs soon find him out, and even so, the scent of false doctrine is not easily concealed, and the game does not go on for long. There are existing ministers who make it difficult to tell whether they are dogs or foxes,

---

7. Lloyd-Jones, Martyn. *Preaching and Preachers.* (London: Hodder and Stoughton. 1971), 53.

> but all people will know our quality as long as we live, they will not doubt what we believe or teach."[8]

Spurgeon was distressed that many pastors in his day preached a great many things that were not true and consequently lured men into error. Spurgeon understood that true preaching is connected with the content of what is said.

Perkins, who lived many years earlier, would have agreed with Lloyd-Jones' and Spurgeon's sentiments of preaching in his own time. He defined the art of prophesying as:

> "Prophecy (or prophesying) is a public and solemn speech of the prophet, pertaining to the worship of God and to the salvation of our neighbor. 'But he that prophesieth speaketh unto men to edification, to exhortation and to consolation . . . .But if all prophesy, and there come in one that believeth not, or one unlearned, he is rebuked of all men, and is judged of all men.' (1 Cor. 14:3,24)"[9]

Perkins refers to prophesying as a public and solemn speech of the prophet pertaining to the worship of God and the salvation of our neighbor. This is similar to what Thomas Goodwin said. Perhaps an argument could be made that Goodwin's definition was formed from Perkins, because he writes years after Perkins in the Puritan era. Goodwin writes concerning preaching and its weightiness:

> "That the preaching of the gospel is an ordinance of Jesus Christ, instituted for the conversion of sinners, and for the edification of the saints. Of the use and necessity of ministers wholly set apart to preach. That Christ by his institution hath appointed a due maintenance for ministers."[10]

---

8. Spurgeon, Charles. *The Greatest Fight*. Abbotsford, Wisconsin: Aneko Press. 2018, 47.

9. Perkins, William. *The Art of Prophesying*. Vol. 10 of *The Works of William Perkins*. Edited by Joseph A. Pipa and J. Stephen Yuille. General Editors Joel R. Beeke and Derek W.H. Thomas. Grand Rapids, Michigan. Reformation Heritage Books. 2020, 289.

10. Goodwin, Thomas. *The Government of the Churches of Christ. The Works of Thomas Goodwin*. Volume 11. Soli Deo Gloria. Grand Rapids,

Perkins, like Goodwin, saw the two aims of preaching as the conversion of the sinner and the edification of the saint. *Perkins viewed preaching here in terms of proclaiming God's true worship.* (Emphasis mine) He meant by this that to worship God, a person must know who God is, who he or she is, what Christ has done, how to be reconciled to God, how to live for Him, what the church is, and all the teachings of the Scriptures. According to Perkins, all of the Scripture drives the true worship of God and the salvation of men. With such a weighty definition, it is no wonder Perkins spent so much time writing about what is true preaching. For him, it was the means of God's receiving proper worship from His people and saving sinners. Perkins saw preaching not just as an indicative but as an *imperative*. He summarized with great precision exactly what preaching is in his summary statement in *The Art of Prophesying*, where he writes:

> "The order and sum of the sacred and only method of preaching:
>
> 1. To read the text distinctly out of the canonical Scriptures.
>
> 2. To give the sense and understanding of it, being read, by the Scripture itself.
>
> 3. To collect a few and profitable points of doctrine out of the natural sense.
>
> 4. To apply (if he has the gift) the doctrines rightly collected to the life and manners of men in a simple and plain speech.
>
> The sum of the sum: Preach one Christ, by Christ, to the praise of Christ." [11]

In four points, he outlined that preaching is to read the Canonical Scripture you are going to expound. To give the sense

---

Michigan. 2021, 359.

11. Perkins, William. *The Art of Prophesying. Vol. 10 of The Works of William Perkins.* Edited by Joseph A. Pipa and J. Stephen Yuille. General Editors Joel R. Beeke and Derek W.H. Thomas. Grand Rapids, Michigan. Reformation Heritage Books. 2020, 356.

(which means interpretation) of the Scripture, using other Scriptures to make that interpretation clear (interpreting Scripture with Scripture). Next, the preacher was to outline a few indicatives, some theological and doctrinal points derived from the text. Lastly, to apply the truth of the text and the doctrines rightly collected to his people's life patterns, which he called "life and manners of men," in a simple and clear way that everyone could understand. That last part is key to understanding Perkins and Puritan preaching in general. They believed these profound truths should be explained in "simple and plain speech." Perkins would have abhorred preaching so technical it confused the majority of hearers yet pleased the learned among them. He saw preaching as involving clear and plain speech so all people, from learned to unlearned, could understand it and profit from faith in Christ.

Interpretation of Scripture

Perkins was dogmatic on there being only one interpretation. Like all Reformers, Perkins believed the Scripture had one interpretation. He writes in a critique of the church of Rome, "The Church of Rome makes four senses of the Scripture (literal, allegorical, tropological, and anagogical."[12] In *The Art of Prophesying*, he conveyed that Scripture has one sense and that the supreme means of interpretation is Scripture itself, with the Holy Spirit being the principal interpreter.[13] He writes, *"There is only one sense, and the same is literal. An allegory is only a certain manner of uttering the same sense. The anagoge and tropology are ways whereby the sense may be applied."*[14] Though the Scripture had one interpretation, he acknowledged the use of tropology in the text's application. The preacher for Perkins was to be diligent in outlining all the ways the

---

12. Perkins, William. *The Art of Prophesying*. Vol. 10 of *The Works of William Perkins*. Edited by Joseph A. Pipa and J. Stephen Yuille. General Editors Joel R. Beeke and Derek W.H. Thomas. Grand Rapids, Michigan. Reformation Heritage Books. 2020, 303.

13. Ibid., 303.

14. Ibid., 303. Emphasis mine.

text should be applied to the people of God. He writes concerning the application of the truths unearthed in the preparation process, "Application is that whereby the doctrine rightly collected is diversely fitted according as place, time, and person do require." [15] He writes, "The foundation of application is to know whether the place propounded is a sentence of the law or the gospel."[16] Perkins, in the application of the one-interpretation-of-the-Scripture passage, used the framework of the Law and the Gospel.

Perkins saw from the Word of God the imperative of conveying the Law and Gospel in application of truth in the sermon. He writes, "The law and gospel are two parts of the Word of God and are divers kinds of doctrine. By the law, I understand that part of God's Word which promises life to the obeyer. By the gospel, that part which promises it to the believer."[17] His paradigm in taking the truths with Law and Gospel in mind was to see the people of God know what to believe and what to do in light of the Scripture that was being preached. He wanted them to know what to do in the application (Law) and what to hope from the text (Gospel).

Prayer and proclamation

Perkins emphasized the two aspects of preaching: the proclamation element of preaching and praying to God in dependence. He writes:

> "There are two parts of prophecy: (1) preaching of the Word, and (2) conceiving of prayers. For in speaking there are only two duties of the prophet (that is, of the minister of the Word), to wit, preaching of the Word and praying unto God in the name of the people." [18]

15. Ibid., 334.
16. Ibid., 334.
17. Perkins, William. *Exposition of Jude.* Vol. 4 of *The Works of William Perkins.* Edited by J. Stephen Yuille. General Editors Joel R. Beeke and Derek W.H. Thomas. Grand Rapids, Michigan. Reformation Heritage Books. 2017, 53.
18. Perkins, William. *The Art of Prophesying.* Vol. 10 of *The Works of William Perkins.* Edited by Joseph A. Pipa and J. Stephen Yuille. General Editors

He goes on to write what exactly was the content of the preaching event and what the Spirit of God uses to transform sinners into the image of Christ through conversion and sanctification. He writes:

> "The perfect and equal object of preaching is the Word of God... The Word of God is the wisdom of God concerning the truth, which is according unto godliness, descending from above... The Word is in the Holy Scripture. The Scripture is the Word of God written in a language fit for the church by men immediately called to be the clerks (or secretaries) of the Holy Spirit... It is called canonical because it is (as it were) a canon, that is to say, a rule (or line) of the master workman, by the help whereof the truth is both first to be found out and also afterwards to be examined... The Scripture is either the New or Old Testament."[19]

Perkins preached repentance. He desired those who gathered to hear Him proclaim God's Word to be granted repentance by God the Holy Spirit. Repentance he defined as, "a work of grace arising from godly sorrow, whereby a man turns from all his sins unto God and brings forth fruit worthy amendment of life."[20] He went on to write, "The principal cause of repentance is the Spirit of God... The instrument of the Holy Spirit in working repentance is the ministry of the gospel only and not the law." [21] He writes, "Faith is engendered by the preaching, not of the law, but of the gospel."[22] The aim of a faithful sermon was the "hiding of human wisdom,

---

Joel R. Beeke and Derek W.H. Thomas. Grand Rapids, Michigan. Reformation Heritage Books. 2020, 290.

19. Perkins, William. *The Art of Prophesying*. Vol. 10 of *The Works of William Perkins*. Edited by Joseph A. Pipa and J. Stephen Yuille. General Editors Joel R. Beeke and Derek W.H. Thomas. Grand Rapids, Michigan. Reformation Heritage Books. 2020, 291-292.

20. Perkins, William. *The Nature and Practice of Repentance*. Vol. 9 of *The Works of William Perkins*. Edited by J. Stephen Yuille. General Editors Joel R. Beeke and Derek W.H. Thomas. Grand Rapids, Michigan. Reformation Heritage Books. 2020, 129.

21. Ibid., 133.

22. Ibid., 133.

WILLIAM PERKINS ON PASTORAL THEOLOGY

and the demonstration of the Spirit."²³ Perkins viewed preaching in light of knowing his audience, his congregation who gathered to hear the Word of God. Perkins' thoughts on preaching were carried forward in the Puritan mindset, as we see in quotations from men like Owen. John Owen believed a pastor existed to serve with the Word a certain group of gathered people. He writes:

> "The first and principal duty of a pastor is to feed the flock by diligent preaching of the Word.... This feeding is the essence of the office of pastor, as unto the exercise of it; so that he who doth not, or can not, or will not feed the flock is no pastor, whatever outward call or work he may have in the church." ²⁴

This same framework was later embraced yet rephrased by Reformed men even in our time. In his work, *Pastoral Theology*, Albert Martin writes, "The proclamation, explanation, and application of scriptural truth in the power of the Holy Spirit must constitute the heart and soul of all our preaching."²⁵ Martin, who references Owen often in his *Pastoral Theology*, puts in our vernacular what Perkins was saying in his time.

The responsibility of a pastor to study

Paul tells Timothy in 2 Timothy 2:15, "Do your best to present yourself to God as one approved, a worker who has no need to be ashamed, rightly handling the word of truth." He conveys that Timothy and, by inference, *all* pastors, are to rightly handle the Word of God. The word "rightly handling" is the Greek participle

---

23. Perkins, William. *The Art of Prophesying*. Vol. 10 of *The Works of William Perkins*. Edited by Joseph A. Pipa and J. Stephen Yuille. General Editors Joel R. Beeke and Derek W.H. Thomas. Grand Rapids, Michigan. Reformation Heritage Books. 2020, 349.

24. Owen, John. *True Nature of a Gospel Church*. Vol. 16. of *The Works of John Owen*. (ed. William H. Goold. London: The Banner of Truth Trust. 1981), 74-75.

25. Martin, Albert N. *Pastoral Theology*. Volume 2. Trinity Pulpit Press. Montville, NJ. 2018, 4.

in the present tense: *orthotomeō*. The word means to "guide along a straight path" or "teach accurately." Paul wanted Timothy to "do his best" to teach accurately the Word of truth. This means Timothy was to be a man who spent much time in preparation for his preaching to the people of God in Christ. Perkins, taking his cues from Paul, had much to say about what it meant to "do your best" in sermon preparation and preaching. He writes about sermon preparation, "Preparation has two parts: interpretation, and right division." [26]

Perkins expounds on the study of Scripture in sermon preparation for the preacher in his book *The Art of Prophesying*. He writes:

> "Hitherto has been spoken of the object of preaching. The parts thereof are two: (1) the preparation of the sermon; and (2) the promulgation (or uttering) of it . . . In preparation, private study is with diligence to be used . . . .Concerning the study of divinity, take this advice. First, diligently imprint both in your mind and memory the substance of divinity described with definitions, divisions, and explications of the properties. Second, proceed to the reading of the Scriptures in this order: Using a grammatical, rhetorical, and logical analysis, and the help of the rest of the arts, read first the epistle of Paul to the Romans, after that, the Gospel of John. And then the other books of the New Testament will be easier when they are read. When all this is done, learn first the dogmatical books of the Old Testament, especially the Psalms; then the prophetical, especially Isaiah; lastly the historical, but chiefly Genesis. For it is likely the apostles and evangelists read Isaiah and the Psalms very much . . . Third, we must get aid out of orthodox writings, not only from the latter but also from the more ancient church . . . Fourth, those things, which in studying you meet with, that are necessary and worthy to be observed, you must put in your tables or common-place books, that you may always have in a readiness both old and new. Fifth, before all these

---

26. Perkins, William. *The Art of Prophesying*. Vol. 10 of *The Works of William Perkins*. Edited by Joseph A. Pipa and J. Stephen Yuille. General Editors Joel R. Beeke and Derek W.H. Thomas. Grand Rapids, Michigan. Reformation Heritage Books. 2020, 303.

> *things God must earnestly be sued unto by prayer, that He would bless these means, and that He would open the meaning of the Scriptures to us who are blind." [27]*

Perkins wanted the pastors he was training to study the Scriptures rightly and receive the aid of the orthodox men before them. He emphasizes the need for pastors to be men dependent on God in prayer for His grace to grant them an understanding of these things for His glory. Notice the detail in the above quotation of what the pastor was to do in the examination of certain books and their divisions. Perkins highlighted three things to employ in the study of the Word of God:

> "First, we must observe the true sense and meaning of that which we hear or read. Second, we must mark what experience we had of the truth of the Word in our own persons, as in the exercises of repentance and invocation of God's name, and in all our temptations. Third, we must consider how far forth we have been answerable to God's Word in obedience, and wherein we have been defective by transgressions."[28]

He called the student of the Word not only to rightly understand the passage but also to apply it personally. It was never enough proper study to understand the truth intellectually. The truth, according to Perkins, had to touch every aspect of human existence and being.

Having prepared and studied, the pastor was to deliver the message in the grace and strength of the Holy Spirit. Perkins was not in favor of using a manuscript for the sermon itself once the study was finished and the time had come for the delivery of the sermon. He writes:

27. Perkins, William. *The Art of Prophesying. Vol. 10 of The Works of William Perkins.* Edited by Joseph A. Pipa and J. Stephen Yuille. General Editors Joel R. Beeke and Derek W.H. Thomas. Grand Rapids, Michigan. Reformation Heritage Books. 2020, 301-302.

28. Perkins, William. *Man's Imagination. Vol. 9 of The Works of William Perkins.* Edited by J. Stephen Yuille. General Editors Joel R. Beeke and Derek W.H. Thomas. Grand Rapids, Michigan. Reformation Heritage Books. 2020, 245.

> "Their study has many discommodities, who do con their written sermons word for word. (1) It asks great labor. (2) He who through fear does stumble at one word, does both trouble the congregation and confound his memory. (3) Pronunciation, action, and the holy motions of affections are hindered, because the mind is wholly bent on this, to wit, that the memory fainting now under her burden may not fail." [29]

What had been studied and examined was to be attended to by the people of God.

The responsibility of the people to listen

In his work *Three Books on Case of Conscience*, Perkins outlined in Book 2, chapter 7, the necessity of the church to listen actively to biblical preaching. He writes in the opening of the chapter a question and answer to put forth his thesis:

> "How may any man profitably, to his own comfort and salvation, hear the Word of God? The necessity of this question appears by that special caveat, given by our Savior Christ: 'Take heed how ye hear' (Luke 8:18). Answer. To the profitable hearing of God's Word, three things are required: (1) preparation before we hear; (2) a right disposition in hearing; and (3) duties to be practiced afterward." [30]

The people of God were also responsible for hearing the prepared and prayed-for sermon from the minister. They were to make sure they were in a posture to receive and heed the fruit of the labor of the pastor's study. They were to prepare to hear God's Word,

---

29. Perkins, William. *The Art of Prophesying. Vol. 10 of The Works of William Perkins.* Edited by Joseph A. Pipa and J. Stephen Yuille. General Editors Joel R. Beeke and Derek W.H. Thomas. Grand Rapids, Michigan. Reformation Heritage Books. 2020, 348.

30. Perkins, William. *Three Books on Conscience. Vol. 8 of The Works of William Perkins.* Edited by J. Stephen Yuille. General Editors Joel R. Beeke and Derek W.H. Thomas. Grand Rapids, Michigan. Reformation Heritage Books. 2019, 271.

ensure they had the right heart posture to hear God's Word, and were to be diligent in practicing what they learned.

He describes several conditions of those who attend the sermon. He writes, "Unbelievers who are both ignorant and unteachable...Some are teachable but ignorant . . . Some have knowledge, but are not yet humbled....Some are humbled . . . Some do believe . . . Some are fallen . . . There is a mingled people."[31] Perkins desired to address each one. For the hardened, that they would hear the Law; for the afflicted, that the Gospel balm would be applied to them.[32] He was concerned for the England of his time and its lack of diligent adherence to the preached Word. He writes in *An Exhortation to Repentance*:

> *"First, the gospel has been preached these thirty-five years, and is daily more and more, so that the light thereof never shone more gloriously since the primitive church. Yet, for all this, there is a general ignorance, general of all people, general of all points, yea, as though there were no preaching at all. Yea, when popery was newly banished, there was more knowledge in many than is now in the body of our nation. And the more it is preached, the more ignorant are many, the more blind, and the more hardened. So they, the more they hear the gospel, the less they esteem it and the more they condemn it. And the more God calls, the deafer they are. And the more they are commanded, the more they disobey. We preachers may cry till our lungs fly out or be spent within us, and men are moved no more than stones. Oh alas, what is this, or what can this be, but a fearful sign of destruction? Will any man endure always to be mocked? Then how long has God been mocked? Will any man endure to stand knocking continually? If then*

---

31. Perkins, William. *The Art of Prophesying*. Vol. 10 of *The Works of William Perkins*. Edited by Joseph A. Pipa and J. Stephen Yuille. General Editors Joel R. Beeke and Derek W.H. Thomas. Grand Rapids, Michigan. Reformation Heritage Books. 2020, 335-342.

32. Summarized from Perkins' teaching on application of truth in sermon found in: Perkins, William. *The Art of Prophesying*. Vol. 10 of *The Works of William Perkins*. Edited by Joseph A. Pipa and J. Stephen Yuille. General Editors Joel R. Beeke and Derek W.H. Thomas. Grand Rapids, Michigan. Reformation Heritage Books. 2020, 343.

> *God has stood knocking at our hearts thirty-five years, is it not now time to be gone unless we openly presently?"* [33]

Perkins decried much of the response of his time and the ignorance that still existed, in his time, of the Scriptures and doctrinal truth. He decried the hardness and rejection of the truth by many. Perkins had a high view of the Word of God and its place in all people's lives. He writes:

> *"And so every child of God (high or low) ought daily and continually to meditate in the Word of God. But, alas, this duty is little known and less practiced. Men are so far from meditating in God's Word that they are ignorant of it. Among many families you shall scarcely find the book of God, and such as have it (for the most part) do little use it. The statutes of the land are by very many searched out diligently, but in the meantime the statutes of the Lord are little regarded."* [34]

His pastoral heart bleeds through these statements, which also inform his view of how a pastor would be treated if he faithfully preached the Word of God.

Perkins writes about what pastors can expect as they preach the Word: "Ministers of the Word must learn hence not to be troubled if they be hated and persecuted of men. For this befell the holy prophets of God, and that in the city of Jerusalem."[35] He understood well that faithful preaching would lead to slander and opposition from many quarters of the world. His statement flows from the reality of our Lord Jesus' teaching in Matthew 5:11-12: *"Blessed are*

---

33. Perkins, William. *An Exhortation to Repentance.* Vol. 9 of *The Works of William Perkins.* Edited by J. Stephen Yuille. General Editors Joel R. Beeke and Derek W.H. Thomas. Grand Rapids, Michigan. Reformation Heritage Books. 2020, 114-115.

34. Perkins, William. *Man's Imagination.* Vol. 9 of *The Works of William Perkins.* Edited by J. Stephen Yuille. General Editors Joel R. Beeke and Derek W.H. Thomas. Grand Rapids, Michigan. Reformation Heritage Books. 2020, 245.

35. Perkins, William. *A Treatise on God's Free Grace and Man's Free Will.* Vol. 6 of *The Works of William Perkins.* Edited by Joel R. Beeke and Greg A. Salazar. General Editors Joel R. Beeke and Derek W.H. Thomas. Grand Rapids, Michigan. Reformation Heritage Books. 2018, 156.

you when others revile you and persecute you and utter all kinds of evil against you falsely on my account. Rejoice and be glad, for your reward is great in heaven, for so they persecuted the prophets who were before you." Perkins understood that the preacher had an opportunity to live out this admonition of Christ and be slandered and persecuted as the prophets of old were for preaching the Word of God. We see Perkins' thought further expressed by later Puritans like John Bunyan, who, in his catechism, writes:

> "'When do I sin against preaching the Word?' 'When you refuse to hear God's ministers, or hearing them, refuse to follow their wholesome doctrine.' 'When else do I sin against preaching of the Word?' 'When you mock, or despise, or reproach the ministers; also when you raise lies and scandals of them, or receive such lies or scandals raised; you then also sin against the preaching of the Word, when you persecute them that preach it, or are secretly glad to see them so used.'" [36]

Bunyan saw refusing to hear preaching, and mocking the minister as a grievous sin against God, yet acknowledged its reality, as did Perkins. Yet as the pastor endured in preaching the Word of God, it was, once again, a blessed calling to be used as an instrument of God for the salvation of sinners in Christ. He believed that preaching brought men to Christ, subject to the Word of God. He knew the Christian life under the Word preached would be a life of growth in knowledge and sanctification. He writes in his work *A Grain of Mustard Seed*, "He who has begun to subject himself to Christ and His Word, though as yet he is ignorant in most parts of religion, yet if he has a care to increase in knowledge and to practice that which he knows, he is accepted of God as a true believer."[37] The pastor was to preach to cultivate such an increase in knowledge and obedience. For Perkins, there

---

36. Bunyan, John. *Instruction for the Ignorant. The Works of John Bunyan.* Volume 2. Banner of Truth. Carlisle, Pennsylvania. 2021, 679.

37. Perkins, William. *A Grain of Mustard Seed. Vol. 8 of The Works of William Perkins.* Edited by J. Stephen Yuille. General Editors Joel R. Beeke and Derek W.H. Thomas. Grand Rapids, Michigan. Reformation Heritage Books. 2019, 653.

was no more sacred duty or higher calling than the preaching of the Word of God to God's people each Lord's Day for the glory of God. Faith comes by hearing and hearing by the Word of Christ (Romans 10:17). This faith that God brings forth is the result of His blessing of the faithful exposition of the Word of God: To present Christ to the consciences of sinners in need of forgiveness and grace. To convey the Law to hearts hardened in sin. To teach the people of God the implications of faith in the Gospel for their putting off of sin (Ephesians 4:20-24).

Perkins rightly saw the pastoral preaching of the Word of God to a congregation as a sacred calling and a glorious task. Therefore, we must ask ourselves a few questions: Do we share in his high view of preaching as being the means God uses to draw His people, grow His people, and drive out the wolf? Are we willing to labor to such an end and to be poured out to see the people of God come forth, grow, and the false teacher driven away? Do we hold preaching with such a view, and can our actions substantiate our claims? By God's grace, may we answer and live out a "yes" to all the questions posed.

Conclusion

Much of the writings of Perkins are spent on outlining what biblical preaching is and is not. He writes with precision outlining what proper biblical study looks like. Paul's admonition to Timothy in 2 Timothy 4:2 to preach the Word, to exhort and reprove, is found throughout Perkins' writings on preaching. Perkins believed that preaching the Word of God rightly studied in the pastor's study was bringing the very Word of God to the people that in such a way, when the preacher spoke, God was speaking through him. The preacher becomes the mouthpiece of the glorious God of Creation. Lloyd-Jones summarizes well the definition of preaching (a definition we see clearly in Perkins' writings and thought):

> *"Any true definition of preaching must say that man is there to deliver the message of God, a message from God to those people. If you prefer the language of Paul, he is*

'an ambassador for Christ'. That is what he is. He has been sent, he is a commissioned person, and he is standing there as the mouthpieces of God and of Christ to address these people . . . Preaching, in other words, is a transaction between the preacher and the listener. It does something for the soul of man, for the whole of the person, the entire man; it deals with him in a vital and radical manner." [38]

Perkins' high view of preaching naturally influenced his demand that men be diligent in showing themselves approved. Laziness was not acceptable in the preparation of the sermon, and preaching as a means of grace demands that truth be made clear, precise, and then applicable to the hearts and minds of the people of God.

---

38. Lloyd-Jones, Martyn. *Preaching and Preachers*. (London: Hodder and Stoughton. 1971), 53.

Chapter Eight
CONCLUSION

WILLIAM PERKINS WAS A faithful scholar, pastor, and follower of Christ at the onset of what would become known as the Puritan movement. He gave himself to the study of Scripture out of an abiding love for the glory of God among the people of Christ as well as for the training of future ministers in the doctrines of the faith. William Perkins' works have greatly influenced Christendom in the centuries that have passed. This dissertation aims to examine William Perkins' view of the biblical role of a pastor in the life of a local church in comparison and contrast to the Reformers' perspective. The goal of this dissertation was to endeavor to understand William Perkins' thought, from Holy Scripture, with regard to pastoral theology. We have analyzed Perkins' view of the local church, the sacraments, Christian ministry, and pastoral preaching. It must be said that though Perkins was widely read in his ministry, he has not had such a wide reading in modern times. Perhaps it is because men who came after him further clarified the truths he expounded. Men who were influenced by his thought further developed his teachings. We can see Perkins' high view of Scripture in the writings of men like Jonathan Edwards. Edwards highlights the aim of the doctrines found in the Holy Scripture when he writes:

> "The doctrines I speak of are those Christians living by faith, not by sight; their giving glory to God, by trusting him in the dark; living upon Christ, and not upon experiences; not making their good frames the foundation of their faith; which are excellent and important doctrines indeed."[1]

Edwards writes in *Religious Affections*:

> "The Holy Scriptures do everywhere place religion very much in the affections; such as fear, hope, love, hatred, desire, joy, sorrow, gratitude, compassion and zeal. The Scriptures place much of religion in godly fear; insomuch that 'tis often spoken of as the character of those that are truly religious persons, that they tremble at God's Word, that they fear before him, that their flesh trembles for fear of him, and that they are afraid of his judgments, this his excellency makes them afraid, and his dread falls upon them; and the life: and a compellation commonly given the saints in Scripture, is, fearers of God, or they that fear the Lord. And because the fear of God is great part of true godliness, hence true godliness in general, is very commonly called by the name of the fear of God; as everyone knows, that knows anything of the Bible."[2]

Edwards' high view of Scripture and its content centering on Christ is surely something we have seen in this study. Edwards, considered by some to be the last of the Puritans, carried forward the ideas and truths taught by Perkins and Owen. With regard to the need for trained clergy, we see the same emphasis in men like John Owen in *True Nature of a Gospel Church*:

> "Skill to divide the word aright, 2 Tim ii. 15; and this consists in a practical wisdom, upon a diligent attendance unto the word of truth, to find out what is real, substantial, and meet food for the souls of the hearers,—to give

---

1. Edwards, Jonathan. *Religious Affections*. The Works of Jonathan Edwards. Vol 2. Edited by John E. Smith. Yale University. 2009, 175.

2. Edwards, Jonathan. *Religious Affections*. The Works of Jonathan Edwards. Vol 2. Edited by John E. Smith. Yale University. 2009, 102-103.

CONCLUSION

unto all sorts of person in the church that which is their proper portion."³

Owen also, like Perkins, writes extensively on the necessity of truth in the preaching being applied to the particular people of God that the pastor was given care of in Christ. Owen writes on the application of the Scripture to the people of God:

> "A prudent and diligent consideration of the state of the flock over which any man is set, as unto their strength or weaknesses, their growth or defect in knowledge (the measure of their attainments requiring either milk or strong meat), their temptations and duties, their spiritual decays or thrivings; and that not only in general, but, as near as may be, with respect unto all the individual members of the church. Without a due regard unto these things, men preach at random, uncertainly fighting, like those that beat the air. Preaching sermons not designed for the advantage of them to whom they are preached; insisting on general doctrines not levelled to the condition of the auditory; speaking what men can, without consideration of what they ought,—are things that will make men weary of preaching, when their minds are not influenced with outward advantages, as much as make others weary in hearing them."⁴

Owen expounds further concerning the capability of a true preacher and his preaching ministry in order to protect churches from error:

> "(1). A clear,sound, comprehensive knowledge of the entire doctrine of the gospel. (2) Love of the truth which they have so learned and comprehended. (3) A conscious care and fear of giving countenance and encouragement unto novel opinions. (4) Learning and ability of mind to discern and disprove the oppositions of the adversaries of the truth. (5) The solid comprehension of the most important truths

---

3. Owen, John. *True Nature of a Gospel Church.* Vol. 16. of *The Works of John Owen.* (ed. William H. Goold. London: The Banner of Truth Trust. 1981), 76.

4. Ibid., 76-77.

of the gospel. (6) A diligent watch over their own flocks against the craft of seducers from without, or the springing up of any bitter root of error among themselves. (7) A concurrent assistance with the elders and messengers of other churches with whom they are in communion, in the declaration of the faith they all profess."[5]

Owen also writes:

"Let the ministers engage themselves in a special manner to watch over his flock, every one according to his abilities, both in teaching, exhorting, and ruling, so often as occasion shall be administered, for things that contain ecclesiastical rule and church order; acting jointly and as in a classical combination, and putting forth all authority that such cases are intrusted with."[6]

If Owen wrote near the end of the Puritan era, standing tall as their leading theologian, it seems he is standing to such a height because he is blessed to stand on the shoulders of men like Perkins before him. Perkins' emphasis on the preaching of the Word was something that the majority of the Puritans shared. Thomas Goodwin writes:

"Hence, then, learn that ministers are to employ their gifts and ministry for the conversion of them without, as well as to build up the saints of their particular charge. Even pastor and teachers are to mind this, for you see they are thereunto appointed; neither can or should any particular church engross the gifts of their ministers to their own use only."[7]

---

5. Owen, John. *True Nature of a Gospel Church*. Vol. 16. of *The Works of John Owen*. (ed. William H. Goold. London: The Banner of Truth Trust. 1981), 82-83.

6. Owen, John. *A Country Essay: For the Practice of Church Government*. Vol. 8. of *The Works of John Owen*. (ed. William H. Goold. London: The Banner of Truth Trust. 1982), 51.

7. Goodwin, Thomas. *The Government of the Churches of Christ*. *The Works of Thomas Goodwin*. Volume 11. Soli Deo Gloria. Grand Rapids, Michigan. 2021, 369.

CONCLUSION

Goodwin understood, as Perkins did before him, that faithful pastoral preaching was vital to garnish repentance, growth, and safeguarding of sheep. It prevented errors in the church from arising and permeating. He goes on to write, "The ministry is necessary to prevent errors and mischiefs."[8]

What can we take away from the volumes of Perkins' writings on the ministry? Perhaps a higher view of the local church, greater respect for the office and duties of the ministry, the importance of the sacraments to sustain God's people's faith, and of course, the need for faithful pastoral preaching in our age. May God grant us greater adherence to His Word in these areas as He did in generations past, all for His glory.

To outline and summarize William Perkins' pastoral theology, we must see the emphasis on the necessity of faithful preaching, the faithful administration of the sacraments, and love for the people of God in all his works. The biblical imperatives concerning the preached Word, guarding the flock, and administering the sacraments is a needed reminder for our time where preaching has been replaced with speeches or skits, gimmicks for getting as many people into the doors as possible, and administration of the sacraments with negligence toward all that is holy in the church. Today the call to lose one's life in service of Christ in the ministry needs to be trumpeted. Faithful men should be pursued to pass the good deposit on to other faithful men. Biblical churches should be fought for and preserved, all to the glory of God. Perhaps in such a dissertation, it would be fitting to end with Perkins' exposition of such a need in his time. He writes about a faithful (true) minister:

He writes in his discourse on the office of the minister:

> "First, a true minister may and must declare unto a sinful man where righteousness is to be found, namely, in 'Jesus Christ the righteous.' Second, how that righteousness may be obtained, namely, by doing two duties: (1) by denying and disclaiming his own righteousness, and that is done by

---

8. Goodwin, Thomas. *The Government of the Churches of Christ. The Works of Thomas Goodwin.* Volume 11. Soli Deo Gloria. Grand Rapids, Michigan. 2021, 373.

repentance; (2) by claiming and cleaving to Christ's righteousness, and that is done by faith. Third, a true minister may and must 'declare this righteousness to him.' First publish and proclaim that it is ready to be bestowed on every sinner who will thus apprehend it, and that is able to justify and save him . . . Besides declaration and testification, he is to maintain this truth and this righteousness against all gainsayers, against the power of darkness and all the gates of hell, that this is true and perfect righteousness to him who apprehends it, as afore is laid down. And this is so infallible to every soul who repents and believes." [9]

Oh, for the grace of God to be a faithful and true minister of the Lord Jesus!

---

9. Perkins, William. *Calling of the Ministry. Vol. 10 of The Works of William Perkins.* Edited by Joseph A. Pipa and J. Stephen Yuille. General Editors Joel R. Beeke and Derek W.H. Thomas. Grand Rapids, Michigan. Reformation Heritage Books. 2020, 218.

BIBLIOGRAPHY

Allen, Lewis. *The Preacher's Catechism*. Wheaton, IL: Crossway. 2018.
Ballitch, Andrew S. *Not to Behold Faith, But the Object of Faith: The Effect of William Perkins Doctrine of the Atonement on his Preaching of Assurance.* Themelios. Volume 40. Issue 3.
Barrett, Matthew. Michael A. G. Haykin. *Owen on the Christian Life: Living for the Glory of God in Christ.* Wheaton, IL: Crossway. 2015.
Breward, Ian. *The Significance of William Perkins.* JRH 4. 1996.113-116.
Beeke, Joel R. and Greg Salazar, eds. William Perkins: *Architect of Puritanism.* Grand Rapids, MI. Reformation Heritage Books. 2019.
Bridges, Charles. *The Christian Ministry.* The Banner of Truth Trust. Carlisle, PA. 1967.
Bunyan, John. *Instruction for the Ignorant. The Works of John Bunyan.* Volume 2. Banner of Truth. Carlisle, PA. 2021.
Calvin, John. *Institutes of the Christian Religion.* Translated by Henry Beveridge. Peabody, MA. Hendrickson. 2008.
Calvin, John. *Institutes of the Christian Religion.* Translated by Henry Beveridge. John Calvin: Institutes of the Christian Religion—Christian Classics Ethereal Library (ccel.org). Chapter 14. Section 1, 20.
Calvin, John. *Romans. Calvin's Commentaries.* Translated from the Original Latin by the Reverend William Pringle. Grand Rapids, MI. 1981.
Catholic Catechism. Catechism of the Catholic Church—IntraText (vatican.va). Baptism and the Economy of Salvation.
Catholic Catechism. Catechism of the Catholic Church—IntraText (vatican.va). Eucharist and the Economy of Salvation.
Catholic Catechism. Catechism of the Catholic Church—IntraText (vatican.va). The Sacramental Sacrifice Thanksgiving, Memorial, Presence.
Edwards, Jonathan. *Religious Affections. The Works of Jonathan Edwards.* Vol 2. Edited by John E. Smith. Yale University. 2009.
Goodwin, Thomas. *The Government of the Churches of Christ. The Works of Thomas Goodwin.* Volume 11. Soli Deo Gloria. Grand Rapids, MI. 2021.

BIBLIOGRAPHY

Lloyd-Jones, Martyn. *Preaching and Preachers*. London, England: Hodder and Stoughton. 1971.

Lane, Tony. Review of Calvin and the Sabbath by Richard Gaffin. Themelios. Volume 25. Issue 3.

Martin, Albert N. *Pastoral Theology*. Volume 1. Trinity Pulpit Press. Montville, NJ. 2018.

Martin, Albert N. *Pastoral Theology*. Volume 2. Trinity Pulpit Press. Montville, NJ. 2018.

Muller, Richard A. *Christ and Decree: Christology and Predestination from Calvin to Perkins*. Grand Rapids, MI: Baker Academic.2008.

Muller, Richard A. *Grace and Freedom. William Perkins and the Early Modern Reformed Understanding of Divine Grace and Free Will*. Oxford, England. Oxford University Press. 2020.

Muller, Richard A. *Post Reformation Reformed Dogmatics*. Vol 1-4. Grand Rapids, MI: Baker Academic.2003.

Owen, John. *The Church and the Bible—The True Nature of a Gospel Church*. Vol.16. of *The Works of John Owen*. Edited by William H Goold. London: The Banner of Truth Trust. 1981.

Owen, John. Sermons. *A Country Essay: For the Practice of Church Government*. Vol. 8. of The Works of John Owen. Edited by William H. Goold. London: The Banner of Truth Trust. 1982.

Owen, John. *Eschol, A Cluster of the Fruit of Canaan: Mutual Duties of a Church Fellowship*. Vol.13. of *The Works of John Owen*. Edited by William H Goold. London: The Banner of Truth Trust. 1983.

Packer, J.I. *Puritan Portraits*. Christian Focus. Fearn, Ross-shire. United Kingdom. 2012.

Payne, Matthew N. 'William Perkins's Doctrines of Faith and Assurance through the Lens of Early-Modern Faculty Psychology'. Westminster Theological Journal (Fall 2020)

Perkins, William. *The Labors of a Godly and Learned Divine, William Perkins. Including Previously Unpublished Sermons*. Edited by Matthew N. Payne and J. Stephen Yuille. Grand Rapids, MI: Reformation Heritage Books, forthcoming 2022.

Perkins, William. *Digest or Harmony of the Old and New Testaments. Vol. 1 of The Works of William Perkins*. Edited by J. Stephen Yuille. General Editors Joel R. Beeke and Derek W.H. Thomas. Grand Rapids, MI. Reformation Heritage Books. 2014.

Perkins, William. *Combat between Christ and the Devil: Matthew 4:1-11. Vol. 1 of The Works of William Perkins*. Edited by J. Stephen Yuille. General Editors Joel R. Beeke and Derek W.H. Thomas. Grand Rapids, MI. Reformation Heritage Books. 2014.

Perkins, William. *Sermon on the Mount: Matthew 5-7. Vol. 1 of The Works of William Perkins*. Edited by J. Stephen Yuille. General Editors Joel R. Beeke and Derek W.H. Thomas. Grand Rapids, MI. Reformation Heritage Books. 2014.

BIBLIOGRAPHY

Perkins, William. *Commentary on Galatians*. Vol. 2 of *The Works of William Perkins*. Edited by Paul M. Smalley. General Editors Joel R. Beeke and Derek W.H. Thomas. Grand Rapids, MI. Reformation Heritage Books. 2015.

Perkins, William. *Commentary on Hebrews 11*. Vol. 3 of *The Works of William Perkins*. Edited by Randall J. Pederson and Ryan Hurd. General Editors Joel R. Beeke and Derek W.H. Thomas. Grand Rapids, MI. Reformation Heritage Books. 2017.

Perkins, William. *Exposition of Jude*. Vol. 4 of *The Works of William Perkins*. Edited by J. Stephen Yuille. General Editors Joel R. Beeke and Derek W.H. Thomas. Grand Rapids, MI. Reformation Heritage Books. 2017.

Perkins, William. *Exposition of Revelation 1-3*. Vol. 4 of *The Works of William Perkins*. Edited by J. Stephen Yuille. General Editors Joel R. Beeke and Derek W.H. Thomas. Grand Rapids, MI. Reformation Heritage Books. 2017.

Perkins, William. *The Foundation of the Christian Religion*. Vol. 5 of *The Works of William Perkins*. Edited by Ryan Hurd. General Editors Joel R. Beeke and Derek W.H. Thomas. Grand Rapids, MI. Reformation Heritage Books. 2017.

Perkins, William. *Exposition of the Creed*. Vol. 5 of *The Works of William Perkins*. Edited by Ryan Hurd. General Editors Joel R. Beeke and Derek W.H. Thomas. Grand Rapids, MI. Reformation Heritage Books. 2017.

Perkins, William. *Exposition of the Lord's Prayer*. Vol. 5 of *The Works of William Perkins*. Edited by Ryan Hurd. General Editors Joel R. Beeke and Derek W.H. Thomas. Grand Rapids, MI. Reformation Heritage Books. 2017.

Perkins, William. *Golden Chain*. Vol. 6 of *The Works of William Perkins*. Edited by Joel R. Beek and Greg A. Salazar. General Editors Joel R. Beeke and Derek W.H. Thomas. Grand Rapids, MI. Reformation Heritage Books. 2018.

Perkins, William. *Manner and Order of Predestination*. Vol. 6 of *The Works of William Perkins*. Edited by Joel R. Beek and Greg A. Salazar. General Editors Joel R. Beeke and Derek W.H. Thomas. Grand Rapids, MI. Reformation Heritage Books. 2018.

Perkins, William. *Treatise on God's Free Grace and Man's Free Will*. Vol. 6 of *The Works of William Perkins*. Edited by Joel R. Beek and Greg A. Salazar. General Editors Joel R. Beeke and Derek W.H. Thomas. Grand Rapids, MI. Reformation Heritage Books. 2018.

Perkins, William. *Reformed Catholic*. Vol. 7 of *The Works of William Perkins*. Edited by Shawn D. Wright and Andrew S. Ballitch. General Editors Joel R. Beeke and Derek W.H. Thomas. Grand Rapids, MI. Reformation Heritage Books. 2019.

Perkins, William. *Problem of the Forged Catholicism*. Vol. 7 of *The Works of William Perkins*. Edited by Shawn D. Wright and Andrew S. Ballitch. General Editors Joel R. Beeke and Derek W.H. Thomas. Grand Rapids, MI. Reformation Heritage Books. 2019.

Perkins, William. *Warning against Idolatry.* Vol. 7 of *The Works of William Perkins.* Edited by Shawn D. Wright and Andrew S. Ballitch. General Editors Joel R. Beeke and Derek W.H. Thomas. Grand Rapids, MI. Reformation Heritage Books. 2019.

Perkins, William. *Discourse on Conscience.* Vol. 8 of *The Works of William Perkins.* Edited by J. Stephen Yuille. General Editors Joel R. Beeke and Derek W.H. Thomas. Grand Rapids, MI. Reformation Heritage Books. 2019.

Perkins, William. *Three Books on Case of Conscience.* Vol. 8 of *The Works of William Perkins.* Edited by J. Stephen Yuille. General Editors Joel R. Beeke and Derek W.H. Thomas. Grand Rapids, MI. Reformation Heritage Books. 2019.

Perkins, William. *Treatise Whether a Man is in Damnation or Grace.* Vol. 8 of *The Works of William Perkins* Edited by J. Stephen Yuille. General Editors Joel R. Beeke and Derek W.H. Thomas. Grand Rapids, MI. Reformation Heritage Books. 2019.

Perkins, William. *Grain of Mustard Seed.* Vol. 8 of *The Works of William Perkins.* Edited by J. Stephen Yuille. General Editors Joel R. Beeke and Derek W.H. Thomas. Grand Rapids, MI. Reformation Heritage Books. 2019.

Perkins, William. *True Manner of Knowing Christ Crucified.* Vol. 9 of *The Works of William Perkins.* Edited by J. Stephen Yuille. General Editors Joel R. Beeke and Derek W.H. Thomas. Grand Rapids, MI. Reformation Heritage Books. 2020.

Perkins, William. *The Epistle Dedicatory.* Vol. 9 of *The Works of William Perkins.* Edited by J. Stephen Yuille. General Editors Joel R. Beeke and Derek W.H. Thomas. Grand Rapids, MI. Reformation Heritage Books. 2020.

Perkins, William. *Exhortation to Repentance.* Vol. 9 of *The Works of William Perkins.* Zephaniah 2:1-2. Edited by J. Stephen Yuille. General Editors Joel R. Beeke and Derek W.H. Thomas. Grand Rapids, MI. Reformation Heritage Books. 2020.

Perkins, William. *Nature and Practice of Repentance.* Vol. 9 of *The Works of William Perkins.* Edited by J. Stephen Yuille. General Editors Joel R. Beeke and Derek W.H. Thomas. Grand Rapids, MI. Reformation Heritage Books. 2020.

Perkins, William. *Combat of the Flesh and Spirit.* Vol. 9 of *The Works of William Perkins.* Edited by J. Stephen Yuille. General Editors Joel R. Beeke and Derek W.H. Thomas. Grand Rapids, MI. Reformation Heritage Books. 2020.

Perkins, William. *Man's Imagination.* Vol. 9 of *The Works of William Perkins.* Edited by J. Stephen Yuille. General Editors Joel R. Beeke and Derek W.H. Thomas. Grand Rapids, MI. Reformation Heritage Books. 2020.

Perkins, William. *Direction for Government of Tongue.* Vol. 9 of *The Works of William Perkins.* Edited by J. Stephen Yuille. General Editors Joel R. Beeke and Derek W.H. Thomas. Grand Rapids, MI. Reformation Heritage Books. 2020.

BIBLIOGRAPHY

Perkins, William. *Damned Art of Witchcraft*. Vol. 9 of *The Works of William Perkins*. Edited by J. Stephen Yuille. General Editors Joel R. Beeke and Derek W.H. Thomas. Grand Rapids, MI. Reformation Heritage Books. 2020.

Perkins, William. *Resolution to Countrymen on Prognostication*. Vol. 9 of *The Works of William Perkins*. Edited by J. Stephen Yuille. General Editors Joel R. Beeke and Derek W.H. Thomas. Grand Rapids, MI. Reformation Heritage Books. 2020.

Perkins, William. *Treatise on How to Live Well in All Estates*. Vol. 10 of *The Works of William Perkins*. Edited by Joseph A. Pipa and J. Stephen Yuille. General Editors Joel R. Beeke and Derek W.H. Thomas. Grand Rapids, MI. Reformation Heritage Books. 2020.

Perkins, William. *Treatise on Vocations*. Vol. 10 of *The Works of William Perkins*. Edited by Joseph A. Pipa and J. Stephen Yuille. General Editors Joel R. Beeke and Derek W.H. Thomas. Grand Rapids, MI. Reformation Heritage Books. 2020.

Perkins, William. *Right Manner of Erecting and Ordering a Family*. Vol. 10 of *The Works of William Perkins*. Edited by Joseph A. Pipa and J. Stephen Yuille. General Editors Joel R. Beeke and Derek W.H. Thomas. Grand Rapids, MI. Reformation Heritage Books. 2020.

Perkins, William. *Calling of the Ministry*. Vol. 10 of *The Works of William Perkins*. Edited by Joseph A. Pipa and J. Stephen Yuille. General Editors Joel R. Beeke and Derek W.H. Thomas. Grand Rapids, MI. Reformation Heritage Books. 2020.

Perkins, William. *The Art of Prophesying*. Vol. 10 of *The Works of William Perkins*. Edited by Joseph A. Pipa and J. Stephen Yuille. General Editors Joel R. Beeke and Derek W.H. Thomas. Grand Rapids, MI. Reformation Heritage Books. 2020.

Perkins, William. *Christian Equity*. Vol. 10 of *The Works of William Perkins*. Edited by Joseph A. Pipa and J. Stephen Yuille. General Editors Joel R. Beeke and Derek W.H. Thomas. Grand Rapids, MI. Reformation Heritage Books. 2020.

Perkins, William. *Death's Knell*. Vol. 10 of *The Works of William Perkins*. Edited by Joseph A. Pipa and J. Stephen Yuille. General Editors Joel R. Beeke and Derek W.H. Thomas. Grand Rapids, MI. Reformation Heritage Books. 2020.

Perkins, William. *Treatise on Dying Well*. Vol. 10 of *The Works of William Perkins*. Edited by Joseph A. Pipa and J. Stephen Yuille. General Editors Joel R. Beeke and Derek W.H. Thomas. Grand Rapids, MI. Reformation Heritage Books. 2020.

Spurgeon, Charles. *The Greatest Fight*. Abbotsford, WI: Aneko Press. 2018.

The 1689 Baptist Confession of Faith. Chapter 28—Baptism and the Lord's Supper—Founders. Ministries.https://founders.org/library/chapter-28-baptism-and-the-lords-supper/.

BIBLIOGRAPHY

Wallace, Jr., Dewey D. *Puritans and Predestination: Grace in English Protestant Theology*, 1525-1695 (Eugene, OR: Wipf & Stock Publishers, 1982).

Westminster Confession of Faith. Chapter 21: Of Religious Worship and the Sabbath Day. Section 5.

Westminster Confession of Faith. Chapter 27: Of the Sacraments. Section 1, 2, and 4.

Westminster Confession of Faith. Chapter 28: Of Baptism. Section 1-7.

Westminster Confession of Faith. Chapter 29: Of the Lord's Supper. Study Resources (blueletterbible.org)

www.ingramcontent.com/pod-product-compliance
Lightning Source LLC
Chambersburg PA
CBHW071405160426

42813CB00084B/511